W9-DFV-226

THE BRUMBACK LIBRARY
OF VAN WERT COUNTY
VAN WERT, OHIO

SHADOW OF THE HAWK

More than 2,000 years ago, across the vast Ohio River valley, there flourished one of the most fascinating and mysterious Indian cultures ever discovered in our country. Archaeologists named the people the Mound Builders, after the large earthwork structures that still stand as evidence of their former existence.

The crafts of the Mound Builders, unearthed after careful "digs," rank among the finest of early man anywhere. This is the story of the development of that ancient culture whose spirit was symbolized by the fierce and swift hawk.

SHADOW OF THE HAWK

Saga of the Mound Builders

By Robert Myron

G. P. Putnam's Sons · New York

To
Ralph Fanning
teacher, scholar and devoted
friend

Contents

ACKNOWLEDGMENTS

In piecing together the origins and achievements of the Mound Builders and the reasons for their decline, I have leaned heavily on the work of many archaeologists and scholars. If it were not for the published reports by these archaeologists, this book could not have been written.

While many people were called upon during my years of study, grateful acknowledgment is due especially to Ralph Fanning, Frederick Lowenstein, Melvin Fowler, Raymond Baby, and William Webb. I also want to express my sincere appreciation to the Ohio State Museum for granting me a fellowship which enabled me to study first hand many of the finest carvings that had been recovered from the mounds. These carvings are now in the Museum's collection.

Lastly, my thanks to John Hopkins, for his excellent and vivid drawings, and to Arlene Lavey, for her help in editing and typing the final manuscript.

Illustrations:

The drawings in this book were made by John F. Hopkins, Professor and Chairman of the Department of Fine Arts at Hofstra University. Professor Hopkins studied art at Cornell University, where he received his Master of Fine Arts Degree in 1950. His drawings and paintings have been exhibited in numerous one-man and group shows in New York; some works are represented in public and private collections, and he is the recipient of several awards in important art competitions. For many years, Professor Hopkins has studied the art forms of primitive peoples, and in these superb drawings he has captured the uniqueness and spirit of the many carvings created by these Indians of long ago.

SHADOW OF THE HAWK

Introduction

When the first Europeans set foot on North American soil, they found little to admire in the culture of the natives. The Indians wore strange paint and feathers and had never heard of science, gunpowder or trade. They were considered savages. So the Europeans planted their flags, staked out their claims and took over the crops. Then, having taught the Indians the folly of resistance, they gave a little thought to reclaiming them from savagery.

But as we now know, the Indians were not as primitive as they seemed. Man had made considerable progress in North America since the Ice Age, although perhaps not as much as in Europe and parts of Asia. The years had brought an increasing knowledge of nature to these apparently savage peoples, a perfection of their arts and skills and techniques. Even more important, time had brought them a compulsion to ask and

15

answer questions concerning the mystery of life and death which had been troubling European philosophers for centuries.

We have learned of these things much as we learned of the early cultures in Europe and Asia: through objects of useful, decorative and religious art left in ancient burial places. And it is the archaeologist who has brought these items to light after they had lain hidden for thousands of years. He is concerned with these objects not for their monetary value, but for what they tell of ancient man's life and culture. In his attempt to reconstruct the life of early man, the archaeologist must, of necessity, sometimes work with only the smallest surviving fragments of a culture. He cannot reconstruct the language, religion, songs, dances and music of these people. At best, he can only make guesses about such intangible things.

Solving the problem of how human beings lived with only a few surviving fragments — what they knew, what they had, what they believed — is one of the most exciting detective games in the world. In this book we will have many opportunities to see how that game is played. It tells the story of one of the most fascinating and mysterious Indian cultures ever discovered in our country. This culture flourished more than 2,000 years ago across a vast territory including at least 10 present-day states of the nation. The villages and trading outposts reached from the Great Lakes to the Gulf of Mexico and from New York and Pennsylvania to Missouri. The heart of this empire was in the Ohio River valley near what is now the town of Chillicothe, Ohio.

Although the Indians who once lived here have long

since disappeared, many large earthwork structures still stand as evidence of their former presence. These take many forms. Most of them are embankments built in a variety of geometric shapes and enclosing many acres of land. Still others are like giant snakes, one of which is more than 1,000 feet long. Within and around these embankments are clusters of earthen mounds in which the Indians buried their priests and their chieftains. And in the graves of these men they placed art treasures: stone carvings, decorated pottery, copper and mica cutouts, jewelry of beads and shell, painted textiles. Strewn in the graves were countless pearls from the mussels and oysters which once abounded in nearby streams. The craftsmanship developed by the Mound Builders, especially in sculpture, ranks among the finest artistic achievements of early man anywhere in the world. The variety of forms, the diversity of materials and styles found in this area make it the most unusual and exciting early art center known in North America.

The carvings tell much about the people who made them. From the animals sculpted on the stone pipes, we can identify the forces or creatures they relied on for good hunting and a safe return to their home fires. From their clay figures, we can learn how they and their wives dressed and how their children were carried about and comforted. Their ritual works of art show us how they symbolized the forces of strength and reassurance that stood between them and danger or death.

Of the many living creatures portrayed in their sculpture, the hawk was the most common. Why should the hawk, of all the countless species of animals and birds, have captured the imagination of these Indians? First, it was the Peregrine Falcon, commonly called the Duck Hawk, the most ferocious member of the hawk family, and the American cousin of the hunting falcon immortalized in song and poetry of the Middle Ages in Europe. Second, for its size it is perhaps the fiercest and swiftest bird of prey known to man. It can dive on its prey at a speed of more than 170 miles an hour. What creature could better symbolize the prowess of hunter, fighter and protector, required of Indian braves, than this fearless winged warrior?

No one knew who these Indians were who built such great mounds and clung to the image of the hawk, not even the Indians found living near these structures by later European explorers. We do not know by what name, if any, these ancient Mound Builders called themselves. One group of archaeologists simply labeled them Hopewell because excavations of 38 mounds were made on land once owned by M. C. Hopewell in Ross County, Ohio. Their culture has been dated from about A.D. 100 to A.D. 1000. Another group of about the same era is called the Adena, because a typical mound was excavated on an estate so named by the owner, William Worthington, former governor of Ohio. This culture dates from about 500 B.C. to A.D. 500. The discovery and excavation of the Hopewell and Adena mounds did not begin until the nineteenth century. More mounds were opened by the spades of archaeologists at the turn of the century, and the work still goes on.

Many other Indian tribes also built mounds during and after the decline of the Hopewell culture. More than 100,000 such structures have been counted, strewn across the United States east of the Rockies. Many of these mounds can be recognized only by a trained eye as the passing years have reduced them to mere humps and ridges. Overgrown with trees and a cover of brambles, they now tend to blend into the landscape.

Just as there were mounds built by many different Indians in this part of the country, so too were there mounds built for many different purposes. Some Indian mounds were erected to be burial places, but others were of strange shapes and contained nothing. Many mounds in the southeastern states were foundations for wooden temples. The Indians who created these large structures have been called the Temple Mound peoples, and their culture developed after the decline of the Hopewell to the north.

Although the name Mound Builders can be applied to the many different peoples who produced such structures in America and elsewhere in the world, to most archaeologists it has come to mean the ancient Hopewell and Adena Indians of the Ohio River valley who built the biggest, finest and most conspicuous mounds.

Of course the great achievement of the Mound Builders did not happen suddenly. The culture developed gradually in the same river valleys where their ancestors had lived for centuries. Their story, therefore, begins with the first evidence of man in North America about 20,000 years ago. These early wanderers who lived only by killing animals are often called the Early Hunters. Their descendants later mingled with other migrating groups, and they settled for periods of time in the Ohio River valley. Here they consumed vast quantities of shellfish, and in time the discarded shells formed enormous heaps upon which they lived and in which they buried their dead. Archaeologists call the culture of these people, which began about 5000 B.C., the Archaic, and out of it developed the great achievements of the Mound Builders.

It has been traditional, at least until very recently, to ascribe greatness only to the realistic art of the Greeks and Romans and of the Europeans of the Renaissance, Reformation and Revolution. But the Indian, like other primitive artists, was more concerned with giving emphasis to what interested him most and in minimizing or disregarding what he considered superfluous. He took liberties with nature and often simplified, distorted or exaggerated the subjects of nature or parts of them for symbolical or decorative purposes. Thus the art of these Indians is more symbolic and imaginative and abstract.

Around the turn of the century, certain European artists and scholars began to consider the art of primitive man not merely as museum curios, but rather as art in the same sense as the art of their own continent. Picasso, Braque and Matisse, among other artists, revolted against the classical art tradition taught at academies in many cities of Europe and America. The abstract and symbolic sculpture of Africans, Pacific islanders and Indian tribes of the Americas offered them a new outlook and helped inspire some of the modern art that we see in our museums today.

Thus the primitive Mound Builders, who lived and worked under the shadow of the hawk, have a real connection with the twentieth century.

1

A Spear Is Thrown

UNTIL 1926, archaeologists could do no more than guess at how long man had lived on the North American continent. He might have roamed across what is now the United States 5,000, or 10,000, or possibly 20,000 years ago. A greater age was ruled out because no older fossilized bones of man had ever been found. Nor could one presume that the Indian had evolved in the Americas from some kind of apelike creature. No evidence of such apes has ever been found anywhere on the continents.

A prehistoric hunter, the petrified body of a bison and a modern scientist are responsible for the knowledge that the presence of man in North America dates back to 20,000 years ago. The dramatic discovery took place in 1926 on the hot, sun-baked plains outside the small town of Folsom, New Mexico. There Dr. J. D. Figgins, archaeologist of the Denver Museum of Natural History, found the skeleton of a bison known to have been extinct on this continent for 20,000 years. Driven into its bones so deeply that it could not have been shaken loose was the flinthead of a spear. The man who threw that spear brought down more than a meal for himself. Scholars have prized his quarry ever since finding it.

How did Dr. Figgins know where to dig? Sharp-eyed travelers had told him of seeing strange animal bones (later identified as those of a bison) and finding unusual flint points in the side of a steep ravine. After examining the site, he became convinced that its excavation might provide a clue to the secret of how long man had lived in North America. But it took two years of painstaking

Folsom spear point embedded between ribs of bison. (Folsom, New Mexico) *(Photo, Denver Museum)*

and sometimes frustrating digging before his faith was justified and the skeleton, with its imbedded spearpoint, were brought to light.

Now that archaeologists knew prehistoric man had been here 20,000 years ago, and that he possessed the weapons to hunt the large beasts of the Ice Age, they began to look for more evidence. In the next few years a number of spearpoints made in different shapes by other groups of early men, some of whom even preceded Folsom Man, were unearthed in parts of New Mexico and neighboring states.

This early bison hunter is sometimes called the Folsom Man because the first proof of his existence was found near the town of Folsom. The sharp-edged flint points he made for his spears are called Folsom points. A number of them have since been found at several places in the Ohio River valley. They had probably been carried and dropped there by hunters such as he.

We can only guess at the physical appearance of the Early Hunter. No trace of his skeleton or even so much as a tooth or bone has been found. A nomad, he roamed the land in search of game, stopping in one place for a while and then moving on. The discovery at Folsom showed that he possessed highly trained hunting instincts and skill as a craftsman — two traits that he passed on to his descendants.

Many of his American Indian descendants are basically a Mongoloid people and closer in appearance to eastern Asians than to any inhabitants of western Europe. Scholars assume, therefore, that the Early Hunter must have been of the Mongoloid type and came from

Migration routes into the new world.

Asia. And a glance at the map will show how he migrated from Asia to America.

The northeastern part of Asia is very close to Alaska. The two mainlands are separated only by a 56-mile stretch of water called the Bering Strait. Two stepping-stones, the Diomedes Islands, break this water distance into still shorter stages, the longest being only 25 miles. At times the Strait is frozen over and can be crossed on the ice; and at times in the past it has been dry land. So today's scholars are universally agreed that early man came to America by way of the Bering Strait. And because of the Folsom spear point, dating back more than 20,000 years, we know that the Indians must have crossed the Strait into America about that time, if not earlier.

During this period, North America was in the final stages of the Ice Age. Huge glaciers, estimated to have been thousands of feet thick, covered the surface of what is now Canada and the United States from Long Island westward to Iowa. The freezing temperatures that accompanied the ice killed almost all floral growth, and life of any kind was extremely difficult for both man and beast. Fortunately the glaciers were not a continuous, solid mass. Corridors were left along the mountain ranges and in the valleys of great rivers, allowing people and animals some freedom of movement. But early man found the North American climate as inhospitable as the climate he had left behind in Asia.

The gradual populating of the Americas apparently went on for a very long time and involved various groups of differing physical types. They must have journeyed in very small groups. Perhaps, almost certainly, they spoke many different languages, although we do not know what they were.

The early hunters from Asia followed the trail of deer, bison and other animals on whose flesh they depended for food and whose skins protected them against the bitter cold. Once in Alaska, they found their way southward across the frozen tundra of Canada into the cone-bearing forests of the Great Plains. From here they spread out in many directions across our country. Others pushed southward into Texas and across the mountains, dangerous jungles and dense forests of Mexico. They must have been straggling groups, a few here and a few there, always moving, spreading, discovering. Moving ever onward, they funneled through the narrow neck of Panama and down into South America.

Finally, centuries later, some of these Indians stood on the cold, dreary tip of South America known as Tierra del Fuego. They looked off into the antarctic seas of the South Pole just as their ancestors had stood in Asia and looked into the frozen wastes of North America. We cannot even attempt to estimate how many centuries it must have taken for mankind's dawdling and circuitous journey from the Bering Strait to Tierra del Fuego.

We must remember that these people had no compass to guide them to the more pleasant regions lying southward. They had no idea, in fact, where the south lay or that life was more comfortable there. They probably moved in this direction because they lived from the animals they killed, and the animals in turn lived off the vegetation. So vegetation lured both man and beast from the barren northlands to the tropical jungles of

South America. For the most part the trails of these ancient Americans have vanished as completely as the smoke of their campfires. Now and then archaeologists, however, unearth traces of their passing as happened at Folsom and elsewhere.

These people came long before the invention of the bow and arrow, before the domestication of the dog. They had fire; they roasted meat; they worked bone and horn into useful articles; they clad themselves in skins and furs of animals. Skeletons of extinct bison killed 10,000 years ago have tail bones missing, indicating that whole skins were taken to make robes, since tail bones are removed in skinning. The people sought shelter in caves, or pitched camp near rivers and streams. Scattered bands watched the dawn of a new world. They witnessed the slow formation of Niagara Falls and the sudden explosion that created Crater Lake in Oregon.*

We know well enough many of the animals that fell before their weapons because their species still survive: deer, wolf, antelope, rabbit and countless varieties of birds which are hunted by Indians today. But there were other species, large cold-weather animals that became extinct when the glacial ice melted. Some, like the mammoth, the ground sloth and the mastodon, were terrifyingly enormous. Less fearsome than these, but still frightening, were the musk ox, the American camel and the great bison whose hornspread could measure up to six feet. The remains of the latter, discovered in New Mexico, are important to our story. All these creatures provided the early hunters with food, clothing and other necessities of life.

* Brandon, William, *The American Heritage Book of Indians*, American Heritage Publishing Co., 1961, page 14.

It is difficult to visualize the manner in which men hunted and killed such large animals without the advantage of the horse and the bow and arrow. The bow and arrow were not perfected in this area until the time of the Adena and Hopewell Mound Builders. The horse was unknown to the Indian until brought here by Spanish explorers in the sixteenth century Without these advantages, the early Indian had to depend on his wits, to take advantage of any number of particularly favorable circumstances. He attacked weaker and younger members of the animal herd, or else he drove the animals over the precipices, or into mountain passes where they could be maimed by boulders thrown down upon them by Indians stationed above.

Other animals may have been trapped in pits or tempted into swamps where they became bogged down and a deathblow could be safely delivered. Any or all of these methods were probably used by the early hunters; their descendants have continued to hunt the great buffalo in these ways up to our present century. Unfortunately, none of these systems leaves a trace for the archaeologist, who can only assume they were practiced.

Stones were the only usable materials the hunting grounds provided. And it was through their skill as toolmakers that these early hunters were able to obtain the bare necessities of life. The rugged conditions under which they lived sharpened their intelligence, adaptability and creativity. The discovery of techniques to fashion stone and flint, essential for survival, became a revolutionary step in their cultural development.

Spearheads for killing animals were most important, followed by scrapers and perforators which were needed for cutting meat, stripping and preparing animal skins, fashioning clothes and countless other tasks. Although they were skilled craftsmen, the early hunters were more interested in making a practical set of implements than in spending time on the refinements of shape or surface polishing prized by Indians of later cultures. We may assume that other materials, such as wood or woven grass, were in general use. But it is impossible to say what the objects made of these perishable materials looked like. Only stone has survived through the centuries.

Early man's success at hunting can only be explained by some kind of teamwork, because these primitives had no single weapon capable of inflicting a mortal wound on the large animals they hunted. They probably traveled in small groups, as did the game they sought. Since the game moved around in search of food, the hunters and their families could not live in permanent homes. Home, was wherever they could find food. And being constantly on the move, they showed little interest in stone dwellings.

While constantly tracking game, these people frequently sought protection in the mouths of caves or beneath overhanging bluffs. Not only did caves provide excellent natural shelter, but their location above ground afforded a good view of animals in the surrounding terrain. When such caves were not available, these people built makeshift shelters or lean-tos of wood and animal hides in the open air.

Archaeologists have been able to discover these long-vacated living quarters in caves scattered throughout the United States only because the early hunters were negligent housekeepers. Left behind for the archaeologist to find were the charcoal remains of the cooking fires, discarded animal bones and stone knives, points and scrapers which were used to prepare the meat for eating. No one but the archaeologist, it seems, enjoys sifting through other people's accumulated refuse, but only in this way can he learn how they lived.

Although we can piece together some sort of picture of their struggle for survival, we know nothing about their feelings about death, since none of their graves have thus far been discovered in the Americas. Archaeologists can only speculate about their burial customs and thoughts on death. Perhaps bodies of the dead were abandoned where they lay; perhaps these people were not interested enough to construct graves. They may have had no belief whatever in a life after death, or else held a philosophy in which they believed the body was of no importance once the soul had departed.

Burial customs always mirror, to some degree, a people's belief in an afterlife. Concern for the dead by those who survived gradually grew in importance to people of the Archaic culture. It finally culminated with the Mound Builders, who dedicated elaborate ceremonies, a wealth of sculpture and enormous burial mounds to their dead.

2

When the Ice Melted

It was the end of the Ice Age, and a new world was forming. The glacial ice that had held the world in eternal winter was melting and pouring brawling streams of frigid water into the agitated ocean. Plants that had survived pushed their pallid heads out of the tundra; spores of seeds, wafted on the streams of warmer air, found root, and, under the climatic change, rank luxuriance gradually usurped the place of ice.[1]

If we were to date this change, it would coincide with the change of seasonal temperatures which began about 10,000 B.C. For reasons still unknown to geologists, the weather gradually grew warmer until by 3000 B.C. temperatures on the North American continent were almost the same as they are today.

If an astronaut had been able to look down on North America about 5,000 years ago, he would have seen a

[1] Von Hagen, Victor Wolfgang, *The Ancient Sun Kingdoms of the Americas.* World Publishing Co. 1961, page 43.

landscape in the Ohio River valley area carpeted with stretches of bright and dark greens, the latter the shadows of forest growth. Cutting across this green land was a network of winding rivers; the larger ones we have named the Ohio and the Mississippi and the lesser ones the Green, Wabash and Tennessee. Small bands of Indians moved across this countryside. Some of them were descendants of the Early Hunters. Others were more recent immigrants who had crossed over the well-traveled Bering Strait.

While some of them followed the nomadic life of the Early Hunters, other bands sought a more settled way of life, one that was not solely dependent on wild game. They became food gatherers and foraged for the uncultivated fruits of the forest, the seeds, roots, berries and nuts. Along the banks of the Ohio and Mississippi rivers they discovered an abundance of shellfish. As they gathered and ate these freshwater mussels and oysters, the discarded shells soon formed vast piles. Villages were built upon these shell heaps, and here Indians lived and also were buried.

Each of these shell heaps is today a storehouse of relics of the life of these early Indians. The shells, bones, tools, weapons and other objects they used reveal how extensive was their control over the wildlife around them. Because the culture of the shell people was a somewhat primitive one, archaeologists have called this second phase of Indian history the Archaic Period. They date it between 8000 B.C., the end of the Ice Age, and 500 B.C., the beginning of the Mound Builders' period. While these Indians were struggling to gain a foothold in North America during these 7,500 years, great civilizations rose and fell around the Mediterranean and in Mesopotamia, India and China.

The dates of the Archaic and Mound Building Indians have been scientifically determined. The most common method of dating Indian cultures in this region was born of the atomic age, and it is called carbon 14. During World War II, while Dr. Willard F. Libby and his fellow scientists were perfecting the atom bomb, they discovered the presence of this radioactive carbon 14. They found that it is created high in the earth's atmosphere by powerful cosmic rays from outer space which produce neutrons that react with nitrogen to form atoms of carbon 14. It is so named because each atom has a core of 14 nucleons.

Gradually the carbon 14 atoms descend to the earth where they are breathed in by animals and human beings and are absorbed by plants in the process of growth.

During the life of humans, animals and plants, the carbon 14 is constantly disintegrating and being replaced. But after death, the carbon 14 in their remains continues to disintegrate and is no longer renewed, while the ordinary carbon does not disintegrate. Consequently, the time that has elapsed since death can be measured by determining how much carbon 14 is still present in proportion to the ordinary carbon.

This dating method works best when used on organic matter such as wood, animal bones charred in cooking fires, the charcoal of such fires, clothing, plant remains, shells and the ashes of funeral offerings buried with a body.

The work of the archaeologist and his carbon 14 dating method have given us some idea of a typical shell mound village inhabited by Archaic Indians about 5,000 years ago. Along the shore were massive rows of shells heaped about twenty feet high, reaching back toward the forest and covering an area of more than 50 acres. The shell heaps overlooked the shallows and shoals over the river where the water flowed slowly over rock bottoms, creating ideal conditions for the growth of large mussel beds. The flesh of the mussel was an important food for these people, although among the shells were found gnawed bones of game. Shells and bones undoubtedly attracted insects, pests and disease germs and created an unsightly and unhealthy environment.

Scattered here and there on the shell heaps were the homes and campfires of the Indians. Some of them were merely makeshift lean-tos, others cone-shaped tepees or more rounded, like wigwams. They were all constructed of wooden framework covered over with branches, bark and animal skins. Sometimes the floors were smoothed down with a layer of clay. Inside, the homes were dark and poorly ventilated. The Indians lived out-of-doors as much as they could and went inside only to sleep or to find protection from bad weather. Short, stocky dogs, resembling coyotes, roamed up and down the shell heaps, scavenging for food.

The adults went about their work, some of them wearing necklaces and bracelets made of animal bones and shells. The traditional division of labor between men and women probably prevailed here as it did in many Indian villages. The greatest load of dull work fell to the women. Besides doing housework and rearing children, Indian women gathered food, ground and prepared it for cooking and fashioned clothing and shelter

34

from animal skins. Because of his strength and manual skills, it was the man's good fortune to have much more interesting work. He hunted, fished, carpentered and made tools and weapons. And it was he who felled timber and chopped the underbrush. But regardless of their type of work, carrying out these duties accounted for practically all the waking hours of the men and women of the village.

Some men fished along the river bank with bone hooks tied to sinew lines, while others stood in knee-deep water, ready to throw harpoons made from animal bone at passing fish. Nets weighted down with stones were also used. But the fishing techniques used by these Indians were primitive compared with those of their cousins who lived in what is now the Back Bay district of Boston.

These Easterners let the tide of the Atlantic Ocean bring the fish to them, but first they devised an enormous weir, or fence, so that the fish could be trapped and not escape with the outgoing tide. While construction for a subway was underway in 1913, workmen discovered the remains of this fish weir in the silt underground. About 65,000 wooden stakes, ranging from four to seven feet in length, were counted over an area of two acres. Pieces of wattle — woven twigs and branches — still clung to some of the stakes.

The hunters who went out into the forests behind the river villages brought back rabbits, squirrels, turkeys and deer. And to help them in their hunting, they had developed a spear thrower, or *atlatl* (its common Aztec name), to give them more power behind the thrust of the spear point.

An atlatl is really an arm extender and so simple that it can be made by any young schoolboy. It consists of three parts: a flat wooden shaft about two feet long, an antler hook about six inches long and a hollowed stone weight. The hunter assembled it by slipping the hollowed stone weight down the shaft and inserting the shaft itself into the cavity of the antler hook. A sticky

The atlatl and how it is thrown.

binding agent, such as asphalt, was needed to hold the parts securely in place.

When this atlatl was ready, the hunter fitted the end of his spear against the antler hook, holding it in place with the fingers of his throwing hand. In this way the atlatl lengthened the arm of the thrower and thereby increased the power he could put behind the spear. He threw the spear by jerking his hand forward. The spear flew ahead at the target, but the atlatl stayed in his hand. With an atlatl the Indian hunter could throw his spear farther, straighter and harder than when it was thrown by hand.

Stone weights attached to the atlatl not only gave it the proper balance but also a kind of beauty. At first these weights were simply shaped so that the atlatl would work properly, but in time they took on more attractive shapes and perhaps represented hunting charms. These carvings are discussed in greater detail in the next chapter.

Archaeologists are still trying to find out when and where the atlatl was invented. At present they think it may have been known in Asia before the first immigrants left and was brought by them to the New World. Although scientists are not certain of its origin, they do know that it took much intelligence to make such an efficient hunting weapon.[2]

The women in the Archaic villages had to prepare the game brought home by the hunters and fishermen. Birds, water fowl and small animals were easily plucked or skinned, but the preparation of larger deer required

[2] Marriott, Alice, *Indians of the Four Corners.* Thos. Y. Crowell & Co., 1952, page 39.

more time and labor. After skinning the deer and removing the flesh for roasting, they pegged the skins down with bone slivers and used flint tools to scrape the inner sides clean of fat and sinew. When cleaned, dried and cured, the skins could be cut and sewn for clothing and shelters. The skeleton was dried and set aside until certain bones were needed to make implements such as needles, fishhooks and ornaments.

If the Archaic Indians can be judged by recent Indian tribes, they probably realized the usefulness of the heavy black deer tendon. If so, they would have taken it out whole in two big slabs and cleaned and dried it in the sun. Then they would have split off the tendon fibers, one or more at a time, as needed. A single sinew fiber was fine enough to sew with, and strong enough to stitch pieces of skins together. Fibers could be twisted to make strong ropes or strings for fishing nets and snares and for countless other uses. If the dried fibers are moistened they will stick to each other or to other surfaces to which they are applied. So deer sinew may have supplied these Indians with a heavy twine and glue at the same time.[3]

Some of the nuts, berries and seeds which the women and children picked and carried home from the forests, needed no preparation and could be eaten immediately. But others, particularly acorns, were bitter and making them palatable and edible was a laborious task. First the acorns had to be hulled and the kernels sorted and cleaned. Then the kernels were ground into flour or meal on a flat stone mortar with a heavy cylindrical stone called a pestle. The grinding with mortar and pestle re-

[3] Ibid., page 42.

quired hours of time and the strength and patience possible only to a primitive woman. Yet this was just the beginning of the process.

Acorn meal is bitter because of the tannic acid in it, and it is poisonous if taken in quantity. The Indian women learned to eliminate the tannin. First she dug a shallow pan-like hole in the earth. A dough was made of the meal and spread over the bottom and sides of the hole, as in a pie pan. Then water was heated and poured into the dough. It seeped through the acorn meal, gradually dissolving and carrying away enough tannin to make the residue edible. Water had to be poured into the hole many times before the dough was sweet enough to eat. Brought out of its earth mold, the dough could be baked over a fire into loaves or cooked in water to make a dumpling soup.[4]

In the Ohio Valley in those days they had no metal kettles or clay pottery to boil water for cooking. They were able to fashion baskets from wood, bark, skins and perhaps woven reeds, but these materials obviously could not be placed over a flame. So some unknown Indian invented what has been given the unglamorous but descriptive title of *hot rock cooking*. Stones were heated in a fire until glowing red, then picked up gingerly with sticks and dropped into water-filled containers made of wood, bark or any other inflammable material. The heated stones raised the temperature of the water, and with enough patience and enough stones the water could be brought to the boiling point. One of the hazards of this method was the tendency of the stones to explode because of the sudden change of temperature. Today,

[4] Wissler, Clark, *Indians of the United States*, Doubleday and Co., Garden City, New York, 1949, page 18.

thousands of years later, an archaeologist can recognize the primitive boiling method when he visits one of the outdoor kitchens from the stone fragments surrounding the ashes of a fire.

So these shell-mound people lived on what the world could provide for them. They knew nothing of agriculture; and instead of planting and harvesting what they wished to eat, they gathered and ate the crops which nature chose to plant. Instead of herding and penning those animals whose meat and skins they wished to use, they stalked and hunted them as had their ancestors. They were hunters and fishermen and collectors of the wild fruits of the earth. They accepted the world as it was, and to their knowledge no other way of living had ever existed. That was the way the Archaic Indians lived on the shores of the rivers in the Ohio Valley.

Rivers were the highways of the Archaic Indians, and dugout canoes their means of transportation. Strung out for miles along the well-traveled riverbanks, shell-heap villages were probably united by bonds of similar origin, language and cultural traditions. Each village probably had a primitive sort of government. There must have been elders and a chief who made the laws of the village and saw to it that they were obeyed. Medicine men, also called shamans, must have played an important role in the village as well. While we do not know how much control they had over the living, common funeral practices indicate their control over the dead.

The bodies of the dead were disposed of in a number of ways. Sometimes they were cremated and the ashes either scattered about or buried under a small pile of earth. Sometimes the body was placed in a seated or prone position on the ground and covered with earth and shells. A more common practice, however, was to dig a small pit grave, much shorter than our conventional six-foot trench. In order to fit the body into such a pit, those who prepared the corpse for burial drew the knees up almost to the chin. Sometimes a rope of sorts secured the body in such a position until it was buried. If the grave was not large enough for the hunched-up corpse, the body was forced into it, an action which

Pit burials of the late Archaic period, Green River, Kentucky. The shell accumulations have been removed to reveal graves. *(Photo, University of Kentucky)*

would account for the strange, contorted positions of some skeletons as they were first seen by archaeologists. Some scholars believe that the dead were buried in this position to prevent the return of their spirits to the villages.

Certain evidence discovered by archaeologists suggests that these Indians believed in a spirit and also in a life after death. First of all, fine sets of utensils were placed in the graves of the dead, apparently with the hope that in some mystical way they would be carried into the other world and there again serve the dead. And to make sure that their hunting dogs would accompany them, the dogs were probably killed when their masters died and buried with them or in pit graves nearby. Furthermore, red ocher, a colored clay, was smeared on the bodies that were crammed into the round graves. When the flesh decomposed, the red ocher clung to the skeleton. Many primitive peoples applied red ocher to the dead as a symbol of possible life in the other world.

Another evidence of the belief in a spirit is seen in the practice of cremation. Instead of merely placing the dead in a grave, a large bonfire had to be built to provide enough heat to consume the corpse and reduce it to ashes. This elaborate procedure was probably undertaken for the same reason that it was practiced by more recent primitive people: to allow the soul to escape from the body and rise into the spirit world on a column of smoke.

Whether the Indian pictured this spirit world as a garden of paradise or as some other kind of existence would be sheer speculation on our part. We can only assume that he was concerned with his immortality and life in the hereafter.

Much of what we have learned about these Archaic people came from their graves made in the shell mounds and excavated by archaeologists. The anthropologist has learned much about them from their skeletons. When fully extended on the laboratory table, they show that these Indians were smaller than Americans today: the men averaged five feet, four inches in height, the women about five feet. In many skeletons the bones of the right arm are slightly longer than those of the left. So we know that most of the Indians were right-handed because the arm can only increase in size through more frequent use. A distinctive deformation of the leg bones also tells us that these people usually squatted on the floor with their feet flat on the floor and the buttocks resting on the heels.

The bones that have been excavated tell us much more. Examination of hundreds of skeletons reveals that one out of every two Archaic Indians suffered from arthritis. We can recognize the disease by the hard, smoothly worn ends of the elbow and knee joints, caused by constant rubbing whenever the arms and legs were moved. This rubbing, of course, was a source of agonizing pain to arthritis victims. Many Indians also suffered from serious dental problems because of their diet of shellfish plus a calcium deficiency. Signs of decay and abscesses can still be seen in the rows of teeth. Many teeth have long since fallen out of the skeletons, and in many cases the softened enamel of the remaining teeth has been worn down to the level of the jaw bone. Toothaches must have been common among the villagers.

Aches and pains must have made life miserable for some of these Indians. Sickness, disease and epidemics must have taken their toll; that is the probable explanation of the high percentage of infant and child burials in the shell heaps. But the nature of these illnesses cannot be determined as they left no trace on the bones.

Anthropologists can also learn something about these Indians by examining the shapes of their skulls. They do this by measuring the top of each skull and then comparing the findings with measurements of human skulls of people both living and dead throughout the world. These scientists have learned that skull shapes fall into certain groups: those that are longheaded, those that are roundheaded and others that fall between these two extremes. Research has shown that men of the Ice Age found in Europe and Asia were generally longheaded. Since the skulls of the Archaic Indians are decidedly longheaded, this is considered further proof of their antiquity.

Among the relics found in the shell-heap graves are hollow tube-shaped smoking pipes. The presence of these stone pipes has led to the assumption that the smoking habit in the Ohio Valley predated it elsewhere. Carved from limestone, the bowls are small; the whole pipe averages about six inches in length.

Although there is no evidence that tobacco was cultivated at this early date, they could have smoked other plants. One of these is nicotiana, named after Jean Nicot, of Nimes, who introduced tobacco into France. It is a wild form of tobacco particularly common to the Ohio Valley. Its leaves can easily be crumbled into a powderlike tobacco. Some scholars believe that before

44

Stone tubes of the type used by the Archaic Indians.

he actually smoked the leaves, the Indian found pleasure in chewing them. Even to a primitive tongue, this would have tasted far more bitter and acrid than the strongest chewing tobacco today. But we can be certain that the pipe was the earliest smoking instrument, for the leaves of this wild plant were very small and not suited for rolling into cigars or cigarettes.

As the custom of smoking spread out from the Archaic villages, the shapes and sizes of the pipes changed. Some of the pipes developed by other Indian tribes are called the platform, elbow and calumet. By the time the first European explorers arrived in America, the Indians enjoyed every form of tobacco consumption: pipe, cigar, cigarette, snuff and chew. But of the many ways of smoking, use of the pipe was the most common. There was hardly a culture in North or South America that did not leave some kind of pipe among its relics.

We do not know whether the custom of smoking tobacco was exclusively one of relaxation or had a more profound social meaning. Here again, we can only guess, but there are some suggestions that smoking did play a number of roles. Among different tribes, incense was burned as a purifying ceremony or as an acceptable smoke offering to the unseen gods. It is, therefore, natural to suspect that tobacco, too, may have been used in this way. Some of the eastern tribes did burn tobacco in a little fire from which the smoke offering ascended to their gods. It is possible, too, that presents of tobacco were just as important as gifts of food and shelter. Today, when the ceremonial grand calumet is offered by the representatives of an Indian tribe to a distinguished person, it symbolizes friendship and respect. This calumet might be a direct descendant of the smoking tube of the Archaic Indian.

The Archaic Indians in the Ohio Valley were excellent stoneworkers. They made all the tools and weapons needed for their survival from the different stones that they found. Because the Ohio Valley was a heavily wooded region thousands of years ago, most of the tools were for woodworking: felling timber, chopping branches, shaping house poles and hollowing logs into dugout canoes. Although primitive in shape, these tools

**STONE
GROOVED AX**

**STONE
HAMMER**

**BONE
NEEDLE & AWL**

**STONE
PESTLE**

**BONE
FISH HOOK**

**BONE
HARPOON**

**SCRAPER
(FLINT)**

**DRILL
(FLINT)**

**SCRAPER
(FLINT)**

**SPEAR
POINT
(FLINT)**

Tools used by Archaic Indians.

were efficient equivalents of those used by carpenters today.

The Indian craftsman selected flint for tools with a razor-sharp edge. First he prepared the core of his flint by striking away small chips around it until a cutting or piercing surface was ready. Next he used a pointed piece of an antler as a chisel. Held against the section of the flint, it was struck sharply with a stone hammer until the desired segment fell away from the core. These segments were carefully worked into keen-edged knives, chisels, spearheads and all the necessary sharp-pointed tools of the village. The remaining core was then easily shaped into a skin scraper or ax head for trimming light timber and cutting spear handles. It sounds like a slow process, but actually a skilled worker could make a stone point in a few minutes.

A more durable type of woodworking tool was fashioned from stone for heavier work around the village. Massive axes for cutting larger trees were shaped from hard stones such as basalt and greenstone. Ax heads can be recognized by broad encircling grooves by which they could be more securely tied to the wooden handles. From the softer and more easily chipped stones and bones of wild game the Indians made adzes, chisels, gouges, hooks, needles and many other implements.

As his skills and techniques improved, the Indian craftsman learned to carve stones into many different forms and to engrave on bone. And in time, as his creative talents grew and a measure of leisure entered his life, he began to make objects primarily for the aesthetic pleasure they gave him, such as the banner- and bird-stones illustrated in the next chapter.

3

Banners and Birds

BANNERSTONES

OF the many stone carvings made by Archaic Indians, the atlatl weights, which are also called bannerstones, were the most attractive. Although many of them were shaped primarily to fit over the atlatl to give it better balance, others may have been worn as charms or ornaments. Beautifully carved and polished, these bannerstones resemble jewels in their lovely colors and smooth, porcelainlike surfaces. A variety of stones produced their striking effects, but chert, limestone and flint were preferred because of their wide range of color patterns and because they were more easily carved.

Considering the primitive tools and techniques used, the shaping of the bannerstones was a remarkable accomplishment. Stone hammers were used to free the core that was to become the bannerstone from a large, jagged stone block. With mauls and points, the artist chipped and pecked at the core until he obtained a rough approximation of the desired shape. Then with several stone blades he carved the weight into its final form. The discovery of several partly finished examples reveals that the central channel was drilled while the stone was still in the rough stage. Because of the danger of cracking the stone, the sculptor did not want to finish the carving until the drilling was safely completed.

He probably drilled the channel by holding the stone securely in place, perhaps between his feet. After marking the spot to be pierced, he sprinkled some sand on it and then rotated a wooden stick between his hands on

A bannerstone.

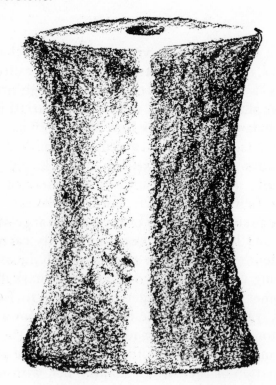

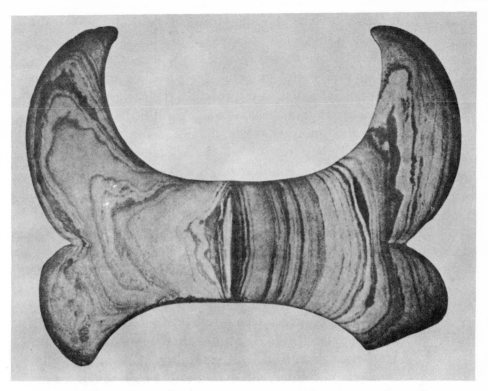

Slate bannerstone of Archaic Indians. *(Photo, courtesy Heye Foundation)*

the stone, much as a Boy Scout would do to make a fire without matches or flint. The abrasive sand did the actual cutting, while the stick merely provided the necessary force. To hasten the process, the Indian may have gouged out stubborn pieces with sharp-pointed copper or flint awls.

After the channel had been drilled and the carving completed, he then polished the stone until it literally sparkled. To achieve this effect he must have used some abrasive such as rubbing stone, or sand and water applied with much elbow grease and infinite patience.

Despite their small size these bannerstones were carved into many graceful designs. The more simple, rectangular shapes were probably the earliest examples, and as the Indians became more skillful they carved the stones into more complex shapes. Some were rounded out until they resembled the spread-out wings of a butterfly. Others had strongly curved swirling shapes. The skill and talent of the sculptors is evident in the clever way they used the grain of the stone to enhance the contour of the forms. They appreciated and admired the colors and texture of the stone.

Some bannerstones may have represented tribal symbols, or served as magic charms connected with the hunt. Others were buried with the dead. These were intentionally broken into a number of pieces before being placed in the graves. Why did the Indians want to destroy such beautiful craftsmanship? Perhaps for the same reason that recent Indian tribes carried out a similar practice. These Indians symbolically *killed* the stone by breaking it to pieces in order to free the spirit or force which they believed resided in it. The belief that all things, whether animate or inanimate, contain a mystical force is common among primitive peoples, and so it may have prevailed among the Archaic Indians as well.

BIRDSTONES

It was not until the latter part of the Archaic period

that the sculptors began to portray a living creature —
a bird. If any other animals were sculptured in stone,
they have not yet been found. These portrayals of birds,
which are called birdstones, seem to be waterfowl. Because of the very simplified sculpture, it is impossible to
identify the species the artist had in mind. The prominent beak, long neck and full body, portrayed as if resting on water, strongly suggest the duck. Moreover, the

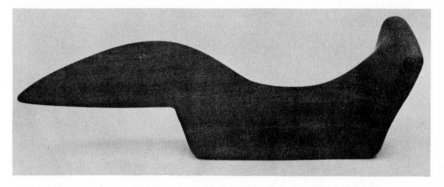

Slate birdstone. *(Photo, courtesy Museum of the American Indian)*

finding of innumerable duck bones in the villages of the
shell-mound people seem to substantiate this theory.

We do not know exactly when or why the first Indian
artist carved a stone in the form of a bird. The idea that
he could carve stone into a recognizable image may have
occurred this way. Sometimes a piece of stone, bone or
shell will, by its natural shape, remind us of a particular
animal. Perhaps the sculptor noticed that the shape of

53

one of his stones made him think of a bird, and he learned that by chipping at this stone he could make the likeness of the bird more exact. After much practice on other stones, he may have learned that he could carve any stone into the shape of a bird without having any accidental resemblance to begin with. When he finally could take any stone and carve it to look like something in his mind, then he became a real artist, and what he made was real sculpture. Birdstones are truly works of art carved by these talented sculptors.

These birdstones seem to have evolved from the bannerstones. Both forms are small in size, similar in style and technique, and both are hollowed out or have drilled holes so that they could be attached to an atlatl, tied to a wooden staff, or worn on the body. For shaping the birdstones more easily, the sculptor usually selected softer slates and shales than the harder varieties of stone used for the bannerstones.

Abstract style is the phrase that will best define the form used in the birdstones. The sculptor was not con-

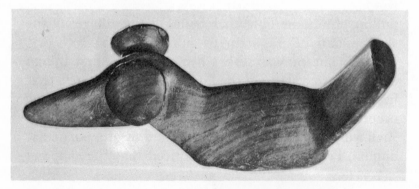

Birdstone (actual size). *(Courtesy, Heye Foundation)*

cerned with the problem of creating a photographic or mirror image of the bird in stone, but rather with outlining the essential parts of head, body and tail. The less important features of the bird, such as feathers, wings and feet, were omitted from the carving. Attention is focused on the head and large, pointed beak. In some examples the eyes are carved as enormous circles that jut out of the head almost like thread spools. Sometimes the head is so large that it equals the length of the body. To preserve the symmetry of his carvings, the sculptor counterbalanced the overly large head with a prominent and expanded tail. As in the bannerstones, the banded color patterns of the stone were used by the sculptor to add to the beauty of his carvings.

In these birdstone carvings, curiously enough, the Indian created a form of sculpture that is not very different in style from some works of modernistic art. We have contemporary sculpture which represents more the personal interpretation of the artist than an exact likeness of the subject. The Indian artist followed a style of sculpture much like that of a contemporary sculptor. Many of the finest birdstone carvings could be placed on exhibition in our museums, and few people would suspect how old they are.

Why were birds the first subject of the Archaic artist? A simple answer might be found in the fact that some birdstones were attached to the atlatl as weights. And he may have compared the flight of a thrown spear with the flight of a bird. Birdstones may also have been created as magic charms. To help the hunter, the sculptor would carve an image of the quarry, then the shaman, or medicine man, would treat it with his own magic rituals and words. The purpose was to give the carving the power to exert a magical force on the bird chosen as the quarry and make it easier for the hunter to kill. This power would have been more effective when the birdstone was attached to the atlatl, or even worn by the hunter.

Although the birdstones may well have been created as magic charms, it may very well be that some of them were carved to fulfill the artistic urge of the Indian himself. No matter what the cause or function of these carvings, many of them possess a high degree of artistic merit and should be included among the finest bird carvings of the American Indians.

ENGRAVINGS

Sculpture was not the only art form of the Archaic Indians. Some artists also made engravings by cutting designs into the surface of animal bones and on the inside of large seashells. Only a handful of engravings from this period have been found, in contrast to the numerous stone carvings. No specific bird or animal can be identified in these engraved designs. They are, instead, geometric lines ranging from simple markings to more complex patterns. The same sharp-pointed tools used to drill holes in the banner- and birdstones may also have been used for engraving.

Three common patterns are to be found among the various designs: the diamond, the cross and the curve. The diamond design is repeated in a pattern which ex-

ENGRAVED
BONE

ENGRAVED
BONE

ENGRAVED
SHELL

ENGRAVED
SHELL

tends around the surface of a piece of bone. The cross is engraved on two different shells; in one example it is simply shown with four equal arms, while in the other example it is more elaborately executed with a variety of lines and fills the whole upper section of the shell. The cross is found in the arts of almost all peoples and usually has a symbolic meaning. Among recent Indian tribes, for instance, the center of the cross represented the heavens and the arms symbolized the four directions. But the cross is rarely seen in the work of the Archaic Indians, and it probably was only a decorative design with no special meaning.

The curve design might also be interpreted as having a symbolic meaning, particularly since it resembles the body of a serpent, a creature that plays a vital role in the religions of the American Indians. It is engraved on a round piece of antler bone, one curved pattern superimposed upon the other. The background is filled in with dotted circles, which might represent the eyes of a serpent creature. Although archaeologists are not sure that this design can be interpreted as representing a serpent, they point out that a similar design was engraved on the loincloth of a figure carved into a smoking pipe by the Adena Indians. The great Serpent Mound built by the Hopewell people certainly demonstrates the significance of this creature in this region.

It must be remembered that visual symbols may be interpreted in many ways. The same symbol portrayed in the arts of peoples who lived in different periods may differ in meaning, just as the peoples themselves differed from each other in their ways of life. Since prehistoric peoples, such as the Archaic Indian, did not leave any traces of writing which might help in deciphering the language of the designs, any interpretation of the symbols is pure guesswork.

Technically, the engravings are generally inferior in craftsmanship to the stone carvings. The lines are crude and uneven in execution. This may be due to the lack of an adequate engraving tool, or to the type of material used — the awkward circular shape of the bone and fragile nature of the shell. It may also be that the Archaic Indian artist did not have the talent for engraving that he obviously had for carving stone in three dimensions, as witness the superb birdstones. Any or all of these factors may be responsible for the meager and unimportant engravings produced by these Indians.

4

Copper and Clay

A T the northern and southern ends of the Ohio and
Mississippi valleys, some Archaic Indians made
momentous discoveries of copper and clay. Copper was
mined before 5000 B.C. in the Great Lakes region, but
pottery making in the southeastern area was unknown
until about 4,000 years later. Although discovered at
different times and places during the Archaic Period,
these two materials found their way into the southern
part of Ohio where they were made into beautiful art
forms by the Hopewell Indians.

COPPER

It was before 5000 B.C. that some Archaic peoples in the
Lake Superior region mined and worked copper. Not
only were they the first metal workers in the Americas,
they also may have been among the earliest in the
world. It was not until centuries later that metal was

discovered by ancient civilizations in the Old World. But whereas the use of copper increased the rate of cultural progress of Europe and Asia, it scarcely changed the pattern of life of the Archaic Indians. They still lived in small villages, and there they sustained life by hunting, fishing and food gathering. The land on which they lived, however, was rich in copper, especially the Keweenaw Peninsula of upper Michigan and the neighboring Isle Royale.

The Indians who mined in this region during the Archaic Period are naturally called the people of the Old Copper culture, because they lived long ago and did use copper in an old-fashioned way — as a stone and not as a metal. They never tried smelting or casting it as did the later metal workers in the Old World. Instead, they hammered it into many different forms, a procedure which did not reveal to them copper's many other potential uses.

Whoever discovered the existence of copper may well have first picked up a chunk from the ground, thinking it was just another piece of workable stone. When he hammered the material, he must have been surprised to see that instead of chipping like stone, it bent beneath the mallet. Copper from this region is famous throughout the world because it is as pure as refinery metal and as easily hammered into shape without breaking; it bends like a hard plastic. Copper ore found in other parts of America is far more brittle because it is mixed with impurities and has a tendency to break when beaten.

The Old Copper people soon learned the techniques of working the copper nuggets. They hammered the

Copper tools and weapon points found in upper Great Lakes (Michigan) area.

metal cold, or heated it and made thin strips which could be cut and rolled into many kinds of objects: tools, weapons, ornaments and fishhooks.

Once the Archaic Indians learned to distinguish copper nuggets on the surface, they began to trace the veins of pure copper from the surface outcrops by digging pits to the sources under the earth. In these pit mines, which might have been fifteen or more feet deep, they solved the problem of breaking the copper free from the rock in which it was imbedded. A fire was built against the rock surrounding the pure copper. When the rock became very hot, they splashed cold water on it. The sudden lowering of temperature cracked the rock, and it was easy to pound the copper loose with large hammers made from stone boulders. The more stubborn pieces were pried away from the wall with wooden levers. Then the copper was carried to the villages where it was fashioned into the desired forms.

Particularly ingenious were those implements fashioned with sockets so that wooden handles could be attached. In some spearpoints and axes, for example, the base was partly hollowed out and the edges bent over to grip the inserted handle securely. To insure a better fit, a small hole was pierced in the base of the spearpoint so that a copper nail or rope could be inserted and tied around the handle. It is interesting to notice that many of the large copper knives were shaped very much like our kitchen carving knives.

Copper objects made by these Lake Superior Indians, whether through trade or some other means, found their way to Archaic settlements located far to the east and south.

About 3500 B.C. some of the ancient miners began to desert their villages on Lake Superior and move northward into Canada. Their push toward the rugged Arctic can be explained by the fact that they were accustomed to the northern climate; when the weather began to grow warmer in this period, and the forests and animals began to retreat northward, some of the Indians followed. Those who remained eventually adjusted to the warmer climate and changing environment. Many were assimilated by invading Indian groups. Although many typical Old Copper styles of tools and weapons disappeared in this region after the breakup of the culture, the traditional techniques of working copper persisted. Finally, in 100 B.C., there was a revival of copper working when the Hopewell Indians began their extensive manufacture of ornaments and ceremonial objects.

Thus, for thousands of years the shores of Lake Superior were the favored mining center for many American Indians. As a result, thousands of pit mines were dug and worked. The surface of the land today is still pockmarked by played-out copper veins.

POTTERY

Clay was the second significant discovery of the Archaic Period. Pottery making is more recent than copper working, having been developed toward the end of the Archaic Period. For that reason some scholars include it in the era of the Tomb Builders culture. But because of the presence of pottery at Archaic sites, particularly those in the southeastern region of the United States, this book lists it under the Archaic heading.

After a discussion of the qualities of copper, it might seem ridiculous to say that pottery is more durable than metal. Yet this is true. Pottery, in fact, is probably more durable than any other substance man ever created. Pottery can be broken, but the pieces will remain intact for thousands of years. Stone crumbles, copper and iron rust and decompose, glass decays and flakes away, wood, leather and cloth disappear. But pottery alone is comparatively immune to the decomposition caused by time. Man's discovery of a method for making and baking pottery ranks not far behind his learning how to use fire.

Pottery making was certainly not an easy task. It required a complex series of operations. First of all, the clay had to be selected with care so that any part of it containing impurities could be discarded. Then it was mixed with water to form a paste. A porous tempering material was then added; tempering — giving the clay a different texture and consistency — prevented the clay from becoming too soft to handle and reinforced it after the baking or firing. Vegetable fibers and sand were commonly used by southeastern pottery makers at this time. But they were not as good as the more porous grit employed by the Mound Builders. So Archaic pottery was more porous in composition and cruder in quality.

Many of the pieces were made with a coiling technique. The Indians rolled or pinched out a thin strand of clay, formed it into a tight spiral for the base, and then built up the sides of the utensil with additional coils until the desired width and height had been reached. If the pottery maker chose to fashion a smooth vessel, he pressed out or filled in the depression in the

65

wall which marked the joining of the coils. This he did with his hands or a smooth wooden paddle. Sometimes, however, he used a paddle covered with fabric which gave a rough surface to the clay. Finally, the vessel was baked at a low temperature, but high enough to force out the water in the clay, remove the unwanted vegetable and animal material and transform it into a hard utensil.

The pottery produced in this way by the Archaic Indians was heavy, thick, coarse and suitable only for cooking or storage of foods. There is no evidence that they also produced the more refined and decorated pottery for ceremonial purposes, such as has been found among the relics of the Mound Builders. Utilitarian rather than artistic purposes were obviously most important.

COILED
CLAY

CORD-WRAPPED
WOODEN PADDLE

SMOOTHING WALLS
WITH SMOOTH STONE

TECHNIQUES OF POTTERY MAKING

Pottery is another invention whose origin is a matter of guesswork; there are three possible theories. One, the primitive Indians may have accidentally selected earthen clays to line skin or basket containers, and when it dried to a hard substance, they decided to experiment with its properties. Two, someone may have built a fire on a patch of clay and discovered the transformation it underwent, a transformation quite easy to duplicate with clay in other shapes. Three, stone vessels have been found among the relics of some Archaic peoples in the Atlantic seaboard region; other Indians may have attempted to copy them in a less stubborn material. Pottery may well have originated in more than one way.

Because so much pottery is found in Mexico, some scholars believe that its earliest invention took place there and that the knowledge of it was carried in some indirect way to the Ohio Valley. Others argue that because of similarities in shape and technique, these later Archaic people learned about pottery from an Asian source. But until there is adequate evidence showing that pottery making came from outside what is now the Eastern United States, the invention can be credited to the intellect of these Archaic tribes.

The life of the Archaic Indian was much different from that of the Early Hunter. He did not hunt big game, as did his predecessor, so he did not travel across country on the trail of wild animals. He was essentially a river dweller, having discovered that the waters offered him much of his food and a means to travel by dugout canoes. Using his skill as a hunter and fisherman and a knowledge of the edible foods of the forest, he lived in the Ohio and Mississippi valleys for periods of uncertain duration.

Because of their way of life, these Indians were never able to achieve a comfortable sense of security. They could not stockpile their food for long; they could scarcely complete a meal without wondering about the next. There were just so many edible foods around the villages; when these had been gathered or hunted beyond a given point, the supply became too short and could not be replenished for as long as a year or a decade. Then there was nothing the Indians could do but pick up their few belongings and move to a more favorable spot further down the river.

During these periods when the food supply could not provide even a near-starvation diet, they may have been forced to kill some of the infants at birth because mothers could look after only so many children while the group was searching for new mussel beds, new food forests, new hunting grounds. It is also more than likely that under such conditions some of the sick and helplessly old were abandoned to freeze or starve. There was probably no alternative.

Thus for thousands of years the Archaic Indians led a life which limited their cultural development. Before they could make any progress they had to be able to cease their wandering, to find some escape from the treadmill of food gathering which occupied all their hours and left little time for other activities.

Although the Archaic Period began almost 10,000 years ago, it was not until several centuries before the birth of Christ that Indians in the Ohio River valley acquired any knowledge of agriculture; the cultivation of foods instead of gathering what they found growing wild in the forests. With the extra time this gave them they were able to build great earthworks, produce rich sculpture and practice colorful ceremonies in burying their dead. This more advanced mound-building culture was that of the Hopewell and Adena.

5

Mounds for the Dead

THE Hopewell culture of North America was contemporary with the rise and fall of Roman civilization, about 400 B.C. to A.D. 400. Like that of Rome, it
spread across many hundreds of square miles and was
bound together by routes of communication. While the
Romans laboriously built paved roads to carry them to
far-flung outposts, the Indians, with less effort, reached
their distant villages by paddling their canoes. For the
Ohio and Mississippi rivers, with their tributaries,
formed an incomparable transportation system from the
Rockies to the Atlantic. These Hopewell Indians also
had a kind of central capital; not a city like Rome, but
instead a compact collection of villages in what is now
southern Ohio. Unlike the political and military strength
which made Rome powerful, the unifying forces of the
Hopewell civilization were the demands of a strict religion and a profound respect for their dead.

The center of the Hopewell territory was the present

70

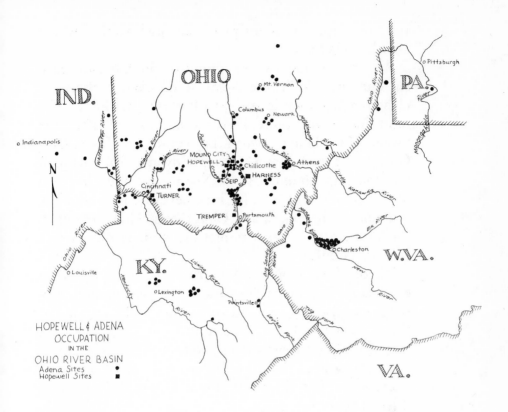

HOPEWELL & ADENA
OCCUPATION
IN THE
OHIO RIVER BASIN
Adena Sites •
Hopewell Sites ■

town of Chillicothe, near the banks of the great Ohio
River between two tributaries, the Little Miami and
Scioto rivers. It is hard to believe that more than 2,000
years ago this quiet farming community was the center
of a mysterious and colorful Indian culture. The people
and their villages have long since disappeared, but left
behind is an earth-built architecture of astonishing proportions. Hundreds of burial mounds that contain the
graves of their rulers and priests, and miles of walled
embankments that curve and bend in an amazing va-

71

riety of shapes are silent proof that prehistoric Indians once lived here.

About 500 mounds rise up out of the flat landscape surrounding Chillicothe. Some stand alone; others are clustered together in groups of twenty to forty. The most important centers, sometimes named after the owners of the land on which they stand, are Mound City Group, Hopewell Mound Group, Edwin Harness Mound and the Seip Mound Group. Not too far away are two other important sites. The Tremper Mound is near the junction of the Scioto and Ohio rivers, while further to the west on the outskirts of Cincinnati is the Turner Mound Group.

All of these mound sites are surrounded by large earthen walls in geometric forms — circles, squares, rectangles and octagons, and sometimes combinations of these. They are 1,000 or more feet long and about six feet high, with gateways to permit uninterrupted movement throughout the sites. The mounds and walls cover many acres. The Hopewell Mound Group alone sprawls across 111 acres.

These six mound sites are the most impressive burial centers ever built by the Hopewell Indiains. In the graves, archaeologists have discovered the most beautiful sculpture and ornaments made by them and other Indians in North America. Southern Ohio was, indeed, the fountainhead of the Hopewell talent, and from here its influence radiated throughout the eastern part of the continent.

Burial mounds and walls were not the only structures built by the Hopewell people in this part of Ohio. For

Four Ohio earthworks. Top left, Hopewell. Top right, Mound City. Bottom left, Seip. Bottom right, Harness.

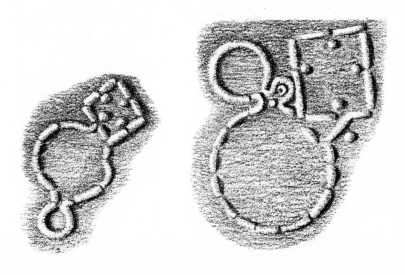

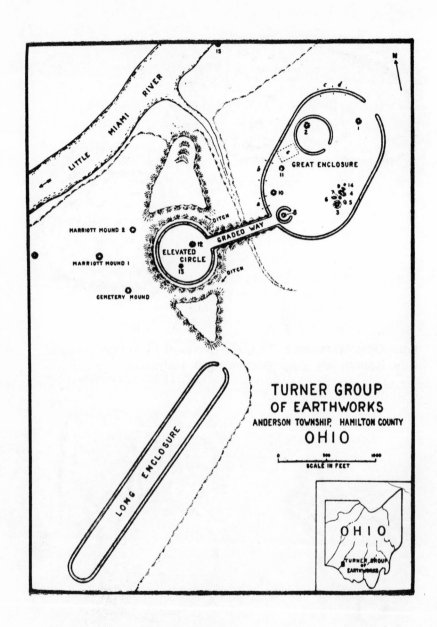

TURNER GROUP
OF EARTHWORKS
ANDERSON TOWNSHIP, HAMILTON COUNTY
OHIO

SCALE IN FEET

ADENA AND HOPEWELL SITES

their elaborate ceremonies they erected equally impressive, if not greater, earthworks. The most unusual of these is the Serpent Mound near the town of Peebles, built atop a high ridge in the shape of the partly coiled body of a gigantic serpent. The earth embankments created to form this creature are up to twenty feet wide and about five feet high. Its proportions are really monumental; nothing like it can be found anywhere in the world. It extends more than a quarter of a mile (1,330 feet), or more than the height of the Empire State Building.

The design of the head, which consists of a series of

The Great Serpent Mound in Adams County, Ohio, is 1,330 feet long. *(Photo, courtesy Heye Foundation)*

oval embankments, has puzzled archaeologists. Some interpret it as the outstretched jaws of a serpent about to swallow an enormous egg. Since the egg and the serpent are well known fertility symbols among primitive people, some scholars attribute the same meaning to this monumental work. Other authorities believe that the oval design is merely an abstratct stylization of the serpent's head.

That the area representing the head played an important role is shown by the heap of stones in the center which could have served as a fireplace or ceremonial altar. On the surrounding embankment, a good-sized audience of Indians could have gathered to participate in rituals conducted by shaman priests, or witch doctors.

Although scientists may never know the meaning of the Serpent Mound, they can nevertheless marvel at the gigantic undertaking. When seen from the air, the undulating body and coiled tail give the impression of a huge snake gliding in and out of the forested terrain.

Other hilltops in the Ohio Valley have earthen walls built by the Hopewell Indians. The largest of these is Fort Ancient on the outskirts of Wilmington. Tremendous earthwork walls rise like a fortification 270 feet above the edge of a plateau that dominates the area. It was apparently not intended as a fort by the Indians; the name was given to it much later by people who were impressed by its fortresslike appearance and its antiquity.

To appreciate fully the extent of this great monument, one should walk along the almost four-mile-long wall that, after centuries of erosion, still ranges from six to twenty feet high. Statisticians have estimated that more than 628,800 cubic yards of earth were moved by the Indians in building it. Most of the earth was heaped up, leaving a ditch paralleling the wall. To make certain that the monument would stand forever, the Indians reinforced the wall with stones at less solid places.

Serpent Mound and Fort Ancient have long since been deserted, and archaeologists have found no clues which might reveal their meaning or purpose. But the leaders and the masses of the people must have thought them most important. They must have felt that here were the greatest structures of their kind, the wonders of their age, as indeed they were. One can only guess and imagine that great processions and ceremonies took place here.

These earthen monuments and graves were not put together with brick and stone, nor did the builders have wheeled vehicles or draft animals. The work was accomplished with the most primitive tools and with the very earth on which these Indians lived. They dug the soil, carried it in baskets and dumped it on the graves and on the embankments, a process repeated over and over, until the massive structures were finally formed. The organization and planning and the physical labor involved may be compared with the effort that went into construction of the ancient Egyptian pyramids. Like the pyramids, these earthen monuments illustrate how powerful the rulers were and the respect accorded them by their people, who labored so diligently to preserve their memories.

The technical proficiency of these early builders was remarkable. Walls are marvelously straight, circles are uniform in radius. The Indians may have achieved this precision in any one of the following ways. Perhaps a preliminary drawing of the earthwork was scratched on a sheet of birch bark. With this as a model and the master architect as a supervisor, the builders could mark the outline of the structure on the ground with wooden stakes. To insure the symmetry of circles, a primitive yet efficient compass of sinew tied to a light pole could have been devised. Equal size of the walls could have been determined by laying down a measured length of pole, or by counting the measured paces of the workmen themselves.

Southern Ohio was not the only center of the Hopewell culture, but it was here and only here that the great tribal earthworks were constructed. It is for this reason that archaeologists call these Indians the "Great Earthwork Builders."

Archaeologists recently discovered another large Hopewell center on the Illinois River in southern Illinois. Carbon 14 tests of materials from some of these mounds reveal an earlier date than the mounds in Ohio, and scholars believe this to be the first important Hopewell area. For reasons unknown to us, some of the Hopewell Indians moved eastward and settled in southern Ohio where their culture prospered and flowered. Many burial mounds still stand in Illinois, but they have no earthen walls surrounding them as in Ohio. Although many people lived here, they apparently were not interested in fine craftsmanship or art. Only a handful of carvings have been found in the graves beneath these Illinois mounds and these only suggest the future brilliance of the Ohio artists.

Much smaller mound sites were also built by the

Hopewell as far west as Wisconsin, Kansas and Oklahoma and at many places across the midwest, eastward to the Atlantic seaboard. These sites were probably trading outposts, founded near sources of unusual materials that were highly treasured by the rulers who lived in the Ohio Valley.

The Hopewell Indians were not the only people who lived in this part of the country. Another group of Indians called the Adena also built burial mounds. Although they had many of the things which the Hopewell had, the Adena products were less impressive and at times inferior. Their earthworks are not as elaborate as those of the Ohio Hopewell. Many of their earthen walls have long since eroded away, and traces of their existence can be discerned only by the eye of a trained archaeologist. In shape their mounds were more like cones and sometimes higher than those built by the Hopewell.

Two major centers were established by the Adena: one in the Hopewell area near the banks of the Scioto River and another to the east in West Virginia on the Kanawha River, a tributary of the Ohio. Lesser centers are situated in Indiana, Kentucky and Ohio; and isolated Adena mounds have also been found scattered as far east as the Atlantic seaboard.

Of the almost fifty mounds in West Virginia, the Grave Creek Mound is the greatest Adena monument. It stands in the appropriately named town of Moundsville. Not only is it the highest structure ever built by the Adena, it is also one of the highest ever built by Indian tribes north of Mexico. People sometimes call it Mammoth Mound because of its size. It is a tall, cone-shaped structure, flattened at the top where it was encircled by a low parapet wall. When measured by road engineers in 1838, its height was 69 feet and the diameter at the base 295 feet. A moat or ditch originally surrounded the mound except for two narrow passageways that led to it.

Unfortunately, the mound was opened more than a century ago by curious inhabitants of the region who knew nothing of archaeological techniques. They dug two tunnels into the mound, one through the side and another down from the top. As they burrowed their way in, they removed everything that they found: skeletons, beads, shells, mica and an unusual engraved stone whose authenticity is still questionable. These objects have

The Adena Mound in Kentucky.

been scattered far and wide, and any chance for scientists to learn something of the mound's original character has been completely lost.

Today, with the very considerable erosion that has taken place as a result of excavations, weathering and general destruction by amateur diggers over the years, the mound is several feet shorter and all trace of the moat has disappeared.

Today's visitors are not the only ones to stand in awe before these prehistoric structures. From the moment the Spanish and French explorers set foot in the Ohio Valley, they were fascinated by these strange earthen structures. Interest in the mounds continued during the colonial days of our country. Thomas Jefferson, before he became President, was the first man who seriously attempted to solve the mystery of the mounds. For years he had been interested in the mounds he saw in his native Virginia. He also read reports of countless other mounds, written by European settlers as they pushed westward across the country.

When Jefferson excavated a burial mound that happened to be on his property at Monticello, he became the first American archaeologist. It has also been said that archaeology as a science began with Jefferson's skillful excavation of this mound. He dug into the mound in a systematic way and recorded his findings in a clear, concise report. He provided a system for excavating buried history, the essentials of which are used even today.

But that was not all. After studying his findings, Jefferson decided the mound had been built by American Indians of the distant past, and he speculated on the origin of these aborigines. He believed that the Indians had not always lived in America, but must have come from elsewhere, and suggested that they had migrated into America across the Bering Strait from northeastern Asia. This was an unusual proposal, because most scientists of Jefferson's day did not suspect that human beings had originated in other parts of the world and migrated to this continent. He was far in advance of his time.

Throughout the nineteenth century and even as late as the early decades of the twentieth, many scholars unhesitatingly stated that the American Indians were descendants of the ancient Egyptians, or Babylonians, or of some other Old World civilization; or even of the mythical civilizations of Atlantis and the Island of Mu now supposedly lost beneath the oceans. A favorite theory of the 1880's was that the Indians were descendants of one of the lost tribes of Israel which had been driven out of Mesopotamia by King Sargon.

Proper Mound Building archaeology actually began with the work of two men, one a surveyor and the other a lawyer. E. G. Squier and E. H. Davis, seeking a solution to the mystery of the mounds, traveled across the United States as far west as Wisconsin, surveying, describing and making measured drawings of the mound sites. They also excavated some of the more conspicuous mounds. They wrote of their findings in *Ancient Monuments of the Mississippi Valley,* published by the Smithsonian Institution in 1848. This work is the first classic study of the Mound Builders, and archaeologists still refer to it.

During the twentieth century, many state governments became interested in the Mound Builders, as have the Bureau of American Ethnology and National Research Council of the United States. These government groups have sponsored surveys and excavations of many mounds built by the Hopewell, Adena and other Indian tribes. But there are so many mounds that even if archaeology proceeds at its present accelerated pace, excavation of all these mounds would not be possible before the end of this century.

Archaeologists follow a definite procedure in opening a mound and removing tons of earth without disturbing graves and the treasures they contain. First the mound is cleared of centuries of undergrowth, and then it is surveyed in relation to the surrounding terrain. The surface of the mound is then divided up like a checkerboard into five-foot squares which are marked by wooden stakes driven into the earth. Along one side of the mound a string is staked down to represent the base line. These measurements are all recorded on graph paper. Then, almost as though a giant loaf of bread were being cut into chunks, one five-foot section at a time is dug out. Notations are recorded on graph paper as the archaeologist's spade digs deeper into the prehistoric past.

Since to dig is to destroy, accurate measurements and drawings of the exact positions of all finds are made so that it will always be possible for other scholars to read about any particular excavation and what was found at each stage of the operation. Sometimes after the mounds have been opened and the finds all carefully recorded, the earth is again heaved up by bulldozers into the mound's original shape. In this way the actual plans of these mound sites, such as those in Ohio, are preserved for visitors today.

Systematic digging during the past fifty years has revealed how the Adena and Hopewell buried their dead. Instead of lowering the body into a deep trench as is done in cemeteries today, they placed the corpse on the ground and built the mound over it. Frequently large mounds were the result of additional burials made at later periods, each covered by a new earth tomb. Most of the dead were cremated, and only a few, perhaps the great chieftains and priests, were entombed in the flesh. Graves were usually made in log tombs and furnished with the finest possessions of the deceased. While Adena mounds usually contain only one or a few graves, it is not unusual to find fifty or more burials within a single Hopewell mound. Because of these large numbers, the Hopewell must have had facilities for storing the corpses, because it is most unlikely that so many people could have died at any one time. Perhaps the bodies were placed high in a tree, as some recent Indian tribes have done, or else placed in a morgue of sorts.

Despite these similarities, archaeologists have learned to recognize certain basic distinctions between the burial practices of these two Indian peoples, and this knowledge has enabled them to distinguish the origin of a Hopewell or Adena mound wherever it may be found.

The cremated remains of the Adena dead were often buried in small log tombs at scattered places in the village. Only the more important leaders of the village were honored with a large earthen mound. Their bodies were wrapped in simple burial shrouds, sprinkled with red ochre and placed in specially prepared log tombs dug a few feet in the earth. The floor of the grave was lined with strips of bark, and in it were placed many of the prized possessions of the dead person. The villagers then built the mound over the grave. Archaeologists are thankful for the fact that sometimes the Adena buried the dead man on the floor of his house. Although the house was set afire and the mound built over the ashes, the basic features of the structure were preserved. This is the only record that exists of their dwellings.

The great Ohio Hopewell chieftains, however, were buried in graves that are the most elaborate ever made by any Indian tribes of North America. And the funeral ceremonies must have been colorful and striking.

Skeletal remains in the Hopewell Mound. *(Photo, Illinois State Museum)*

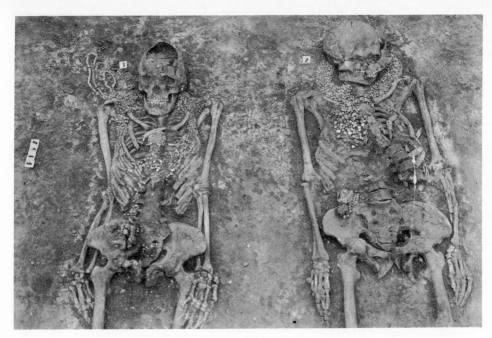

A close-up of two chieftains, showing remains of pearl and shell necklaces. *(Photo, Illinois State Museum)*

First the ground on which the mound was to be erected was cleared and sometimes covered with a layer of hard-packed clay. A large wooden structure, perhaps five or more feet high, was built to house the dead chieftain. Some of these were enormous, like the one at Tremper Mound, which was 200 feet long and 50 feet wide and consisted of 600 posts. These structures were divided into a number of rooms, some of which may have been roofed. On the floor of certain rooms the majority of the dead were cremated in small basins. Because of the small size of these basins, the bodies had to be dismembered before burning. The ashes were then removed and enclosed with offerings in small log- or stone-lined pens.

More impressive were the tombs of those who were not cremated. These graves were built of logs and occasionally reinforced with stone slabs. The body was placed on a shiny bed of mica. It was dressed in garments dyed several colors and decorated with thousands of freshwater pearls and buttons of bear teeth. Heavy necklaces of pearls and shells were hung around the neck, while copper bracelets encircled wrists and arms and copper breastplates rested on its chest.

The chieftain was often buried still wearing copper ear spools and a copper headdress surmounted with antler horns, which was the symbol of his high office. Many of his possessions were placed in the grave; these included sculpture, decorative pottery, carvings of mica, shells and copper, and drinking cups fashioned from large seashells. Some graves have decapitated skulls near the arms of the corpse. These may have been trophy heads of a vanquished enemy, or relics of relatives or friends. As a final gesture, some bodies were completely surrounded from head to feet with thousands of freshwater pearls.

One tribe not only buried its chieftain with all his possessions; it also tried to preserve his distinctive features for eternity. Since they were aware of the rapid deterioration of the fragile bony structure of the nose, they made a nose of copper, complete with hollow nostrils, and inserted it in his skull. In this way his nose would be preserved forever, and that was how the archaeologists discovered him.

Not all carvings, however, were placed in the graves. Some of the finest examples were deposited in a pit dug into the ground not too far from the actual graves. Just

as the Archaic Indians often destroyed fine objects before burying them, so did the Hopewell frequently break
his carvings before placing them in the pit. There is no
way of knowing whether this destructive practice was
carried on to permit the spirit of the object to escape,
or to discourage the theft of these death offerings before
the mound was built. At any rate, archaeologists are
overwhelmed by the vast quantity recovered from these
pits. Among the thousands of specimens taken from
one pit in the Turner Mound, scientists counted 22,000
shell beads, 48,000 pearls, 700 copper beads, 2,000 ca-

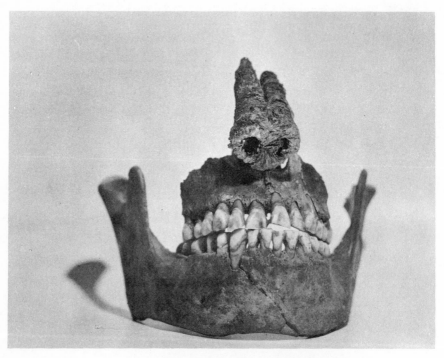

Portion of a Hopewell Indian skull with copper nose.

nine teeth, 600 pieces of animal bone and 12 alligator teeth.

Many months must have passed while the graves were being prepared and furnished. With the bodies of the dead in place, the graves were covered and all was ready for the actual construction of the mound. Some Indians probably stepped forward with flaming torches and ignited the great funeral structure. Possibly the Indians danced around the flaming pyre while a magnificently clad priest commanded the people to build a memorial to their departed rulers. Then began the long arduous task of building the mound; long rows of Indians, bent beneath the weight of their burdens, moved back and forth between the outskirts of the village, where the earth had been freshly dug, and the graves where they dumped their loads on the slowly growing mound.

Religion, based on a profound respect for the honored dead, must have played an important part in the creation of the earthen mounds. Shaman priests, or medicine men, probably members of the ruling families, must have directed the building operations. Like the cathedrals of our day, these mounds received the bodies of the great men. We can suppose that the elaborately furnished graves, protected by massive tons of earth, were built in the belief that death was but a birth into a new and longer and doubtless more satisfying life.

So the Adena and Hopewell Indians prepared for their journey and life in the other world. But not all their energies were devoted to activities in connection with the dead, as a discussion of their houses, gardens and activities in the world of the living will show.

6

Houses, Gardens and Markets

WITH all these remains of the vast earthworks built by the prehistoric American Indians, it may seem surprising that little is known about their houses and villages. There are reasons for this. Archaeologists have focused their attention on their burial mounds and the spectacular finds to be made there. But the earthworks were customarily built on high ground, while the villages existed in the lower river valleys. Every three or four years, when the swollen rivers overflowed their banks, the houses would be flooded and washed away. All that remains of these villages, therefore, are traces of charcoal, post molds of houses, animal bones, broken pottery and other bits of living debris. Only because the Adena sometimes buried their dead on the floor of his house have archaeologists been able to reconstruct it. Traces of the Hopewell house have all but disappeared, but it is assumed it must have been very much like that of the Adena.

The predominating shape of the Adena house was circular, between thirty-five and fifty-five feet in diameter. Larger buildings measuring up to ninety feet in diameter may have served as meeting places. The walls were constructed of a framework of poles. These were set up in pairs for greater strength about four feet apart and inclined outward at the top to shed rainwater away from the walls. The wall spaces between the posts may have been filled in with tightly woven twigs and branches and the whole was probably plastered over with a mixture of chopped twigs and clay for better protection from the weather. Several window openings may

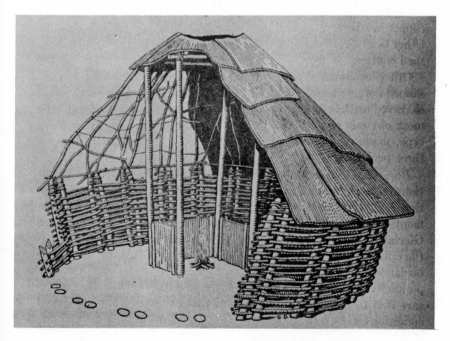

Print of a reconstruction of the Adena House. *(Photo, University of Kentucky)*

have been left for ventilation as well as a single entranceway which usually faced the southeast. During bad weather it may have been closed with a large animal skin. Four to six poles were also set near the center of the house as roof supports. The roof may have been made of overlapping strips of bark resting on a network of vines and sinew lines. A small opening was left at the top to permit the fireplace smoke to escape.

The fireplace was in the center of the house, and it was simply made of several flat stones. Archaeologists suspect that a low wall surrounded the fire to confine the heat and smoke better. The floor was made of tamped earth and sometimes covered with a layer of hard-packed clay. No furnishings of these houses have survived. We may assume the Indians slept on grass beds and used animal skins and furs as blankets. Most of the time they sat on the floor. The deformation of leg bones of many skeletons indicates that they sat back on their heels like the Archaic Indians.

Although the actual height of the houses cannot be determined, the fact that the poles were sunk deep into the ground — three feet or more — suggests that it was comparatively high, perhaps as much as fifteen feet. While not spacious or airy by our standards, it was more spacious than the primitive dwelling of the Archaic Indians. Certainly it was comfortable enough for people who spent most of their life out-of-doors.

Archaeologists have found that the villages were quite large and covered many acres of land. About a dozen or more houses were clustered in groups, and each group was well separated from the others. Perhaps each cluster of homes represented a family, or clan, and each village was made up of a number of such families. They all spoke the same language, followed the same way of life and came together for important ceremonies, and above all for the burial of their honored dead. One family may have governed the village; the eldest member may have been the chieftain and other members the medicine men or priests.

The Adena and Hopewell Indians were farmers as well as homeowners. Since they had no plows, they could not practice large-scale agriculture as farmers do today. Instead, they used simple implements to cultivate small garden plots near their homes in the fertile river bottoms. Here they raised beans, squash and some maize, or corn as it is commonly called. Because these three crops were the staff of life for many Indians throughout the Americas, archaeologists call them the sacred trinity.

Beans and squash grow wild in many regions of North America, and they could easily have been cultivated by the Indians. Research has shown that corn did not originate in North America and that it was brought here from elsewhere. Everything seems to point to the first cultivation of corn far to the south, in Central or South America. It is thought that knowledge of corn and its cultivation spread northward from village to village until it eventually reached the Ohio Valley. Actually, no evidence of corn has been found at the Adena sites, and only a few charred kernels found at the Tremper and Turner Mounds prove that it was grown by the Hopewell. Because of this limited evidence, scholars tend to suspect that corn did not arrive until the latter part of the Hopewell culture.

Regardless of how or when the Indians learned about these crops, they took a long step toward a more certain food supply by planting and cultivating them. As more land was cleared, more food could be grown and a larger population could be maintained. Surplus harvests could be stored away in pottery vessels for time of need. And, with a more dependable food supply, the necessity for abandoning villages grew less. The roots of beans, squash and corn also gave root to a more stable and permanent farming community.

Plant cultivation began to demand almost constant

Hopewell cooking pottery. *(Photo, Illinois State Museum)*

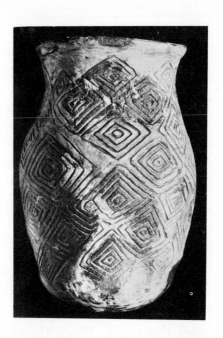

Adena pottery from Marksville, Kentucky. *(Photo, University of Kentucky)*

attention from the farmers. While corn may be planted and left unattended for long periods of time, beans require almost perpetual care and protection from the encroachment of weeds and grass. And only the most simple farming tools were available to these Indians. To make a hole for seed they may have used a sharp-pointed digging stick hardened by putting one end in the fire for several minutes. The hoe may have been nothing more than a large shell or animal bone tied to a wooden handle. Most of the work had to be done by hand.

For cooking, storage of food and funeral ceremonies, the Adena and Hopewell Indians made many pottery vessels. Some of the techniques that they practiced may have been inherited from the potters of the Archaic

95

period. Just like their predecessors, Adena and Hopewell women prepared their meals in crudely made cooking pots with heavy, thick walls.

Unlike the Archaic people, however, the Adena and especially the Hopewell Indians also made attractive ceremonial pottery exclusively for burial of the dead. While the surface of the Adena pottery was seldom decorated, many Hopewell vessels were so artistic that they rank among the finest examples of Indian pottery ever made in North America.

These ceremonial vessels are globular or four-sided in shape with slightly rounded bottoms. Sometimes they rest on four tiny legs. The walls are remarkably thin and smooth-surfaced. To achieve this effect, the tempering material — pieces of old pottery, shell or limestone — was carefully ground with a stone mortar into very fine grains. While the clay was still soft, the potter often folded over the tops of the walls to form a gracefully curved rim. He decorated the rim with cross-hatched lines, using a sharp-pointed instrument, and around the neck of the vessel he made a row of dotted impressions by pressing the round end of the tool into the clay. The body of the vessel was then beautifully decorated with curved designs cut into the clay. The most handsome pottery, found only in Hopewell mounds in Ohio and Louisiana, was decorated with abstract designs of the duck and the hawk. The rounded shape of the designs harmonized with the shape of the vessel itself. These ceremonial vessels exemplify the craftsmanship and high artistic talent of the Hopewell Indians and were certainly a fitting tribute to the honored dead.

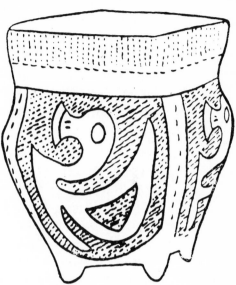

Hopewell ceremonial pottery.

Like their Archaic ancestors, the Adena and Hopewell people also gathered shellfish from the nearby rivers and used the same kinds of nets, hooks and techniques for catching fish. At certain seasons of the year they gathered forest foods such as many varieties of nuts, roots and berries. As their knowledge of botany improved, they learned to recognize such strange but edible plants as cabary grass, pawpaw, goosefoot, honey locust, marsh elder and giant ragweed. Sunflower seeds were a special favorite of the Adena Indians, and they consumed these seeds in great quantities.

Meat was still an important part of the diet, and many animal bones are found at all sites. With the atlatl, and perhaps the bow and arrow, they killed elk and deer and brought down the large but dangerous bear. They also caught smaller animals, such as squirrel, rabbit, muskrat, wild turkey and grouse. After eating the meat, they split the bones lengthwise to get at the tasty marrow within.

The food supply of the Adena and Hopewell Indians was a most diversified and stable one, and more nutritious than previously known among the Indians. Examination of the skeleton remains of these people shows that they lived one generation longer than the Archaic Indians, and many of them attained an age of 50 years or more. They were taller, heavier and more robust. Freed from the constant struggle of finding enough food, these Indians now had time to undertake the great earthwork architecture and to perfect their arts and crafts.

While most of the Indians lived in simple farming communities, the villages of southern Ohio were also the center of a vast commercial empire. An extraordinary variety of raw materials gathered from near and far was on display at great open-air markets here. Most admired of the local products were the freshwater pearls harvested from the rivers and streams of the Ohio Valley. After having been polished and pierced, the pearls were used in a number of ways: sewn on garments, inlaid in stone sculpture and strung as necklaces. Also taken from these waters were shells and snails that were made into attractive jewelry pieces. Then there were collections of varicolored stones quarried from the nearby hills. These were carved into atlatl weights, smoking pipes and various decorative shapes.

More highly valued were those materials which came from distant places. There was obsidian, a black volcanic glass, native to Yellowstone Park and northern Mexico. This shiny black material was shaped into large ceremonial spearpoints. The Rocky Mountain grizzly bear furnished sharp-pointed claws and large eye teeth. The claws were strung into necklaces, and the teeth were converted into buttons. From the region of the Carolinas came chunks of mica. Paper-thin sheets of this shiny mineral were stripped off and cut into different shapes. From Lake Superior came heavier blocks of copper ore that would eventually be heated and hammered into utensils and decorations. Nuggets of silver and gold could also be found in the marketplace; sometimes the silver and gold were hammered into foil strips and wrapped around the copper-ear spools.

Perhaps the most unusual wares of all came from Florida. These included large seashells, still unbroken despite a journey of more than 1,000 miles, which made excellent drinking cups. There were shark's teeth, whose razor-sharp points made a wonderful engraving tool. Unusual ornaments were made from cut and polished bones of alligator and barracuda.

To the Indians of long ago, these materials were great treasures. They were proudly worn by important officials of the villages, and some may have been used in the performance of rituals. The Indians who transported these materials from their sources to the busy Ohio markets must have been considered important personages. Only these traders knew the shortest and safest routes through dense forests, over rugged mountains and along jungle rivers. Only they knew the languages and traditions of the many tribes which inhabited the vast territory east of the Rockies. Only they knew how to bargain at distant places with the Indians who had collected the raw materials. The routes which these traders followed were also the means of communication that bound together the vast Hopewell culture. Like the troubadors of the later Middle Ages, these Indian traders undoubtedly circulated the latest stories and news and their arrival was probably a welcome event everywhere.

Although this description of the traders may be fanciful, the quantities of material found in the Ohio mounds certainly indicate that trading was a highly organized activity with well-established trade routes. Whatever the objective of their travel may have been, these Indians never seem to have missed a chance to pick up something strange. Not until the colonial period of our American history did this section of the country again witness such extensive commercial trading.

The continued existence of the homes, gardens and markets in Hopewell villages depended on the wisdom, leadership and perhaps the strength of one person — the chieftain. A community such as this which spent its life in the open, unprotected from the fiercest changes of weather and at the mercy of the many hazards that lurked in the wild forests, had but its chieftain to rely on for protection.

That the chieftain was selected from a single ruling family is a theory based on the recent discovery of bony growths along the inner ear canal of many Hopewell skulls that were lavishly buried in the mounds. These bony growths, known as ear exostoses to scientists, are very rare; one scientist reported they occurred in only about 1 percent of more than 40,000 individuals he had examined. Since many chieftains' skulls had these growths, and since they are an inbred family trait, it is presumed that the chieftains came from the same family and represented the first aristocracy in prehistoric America.

A more distinguishing feature of the Hopewell as well as the Adena ruling families were the purposely deformed forehead and rear portion of their skulls. This artificial deformation, as it is known to archaeologists, was done following the birth of the infant. The back of his head was placed against a wood cradleboard and secured in position with thongs that passed around his forehead and were tied behind the board. By strapping the skull in this way, the soft bones of the baby were brought flat against the hard board, and as the child grew the back of his head remained flattened, while the thongs gave the forehead a depressed shape. Sometimes the binding was so tight that the thongs left an indelible impression on the skull bones. Even when old enough to discard the cradleboard, the child still wore the binding to maintain the desired head shape.

There are different theories as to the reasons these Indians wanted to have deformed skulls. Some scholars believe it was a sign of the important status of the chieftain and members of his family. Others argue that it was just a matter of fashion or beauty.

The physical characteristics of the Hopewell chieftain were not too apparent. But the wealth of jewelry and ornaments that he wore certainly identified him as the

A Hopewell chieftain. *(Photo, Illinois State Museum)*

leader he was. Across his shoulders he wore a knee-length mantle. It was decorated with turkey feathers, painted in several colors, and embroidered with hundreds of perfectly matched freshwater pearls. His feet were shod in beaded leather moccasins. Adding to his stature and dignity were two tall deer antlers attached to a copper headplate.

His face was decorated with paint and some tattooing. His earlobes had been pierced and had stretched around copper ear spools. A copper breastplate hung from his neck, while copper bands, strands of beads, pearls and animal claws encircled his neck, wrists and ankles. Attached to his waist were ornaments cut from jaws of both animals and humans. In one hand he carried a large copper axe and in the other a wooden spear tipped with a carefully worked obsidian point. He was truly a resplendent figure, as colorful and striking as his Viking contemporary on the other side of the Atlantic.

This description of the chieftain is based solely on archaeological evidence found in the mounds. But the Indian artist also depicted the clothing and fashions of other members of the village in small carvings that he made of them.

7

Figurines and Fashions

UNTIL 1922 no human figures had ever been found among the relics of the Mound Builders, except for carvings on a few effigy pipes. Hundreds of carvings had been discovered, yet none represented the human figure. Scholars speculated that the Indians considered the human figure too sacred to be shown in their art, or that animal creatures best exemplified their spiritual and ceremonial needs. Then a Harvard archaeologist named Charles Willoughby uncovered a number of clay Indians which showed for the first time how they looked and dressed.

This discovery took place while Mr. Willoughby was digging into the large Hopewell mound at the Turner site outside Cincinnati. A workman's spade had revealed a large ceremonial cache on the floor of the mound, and one by one the objects and ornaments were carefully removed. A shaft of sunlight struck a large coiled serpent made of mica, and it sparkled like silver. This creature may have been a protective deity, because directly beneath it were the sculptured figures of Hopewell men and women. They were the first representations of Indians who died about 2,000 years ago and perhaps the earliest works of human sculpture found anywhere in North America.

The excitement of the discovery was dampened by the badly preserved condition of the figures. They were broken, and none was complete. Like the effigy pipes, they apparently had been ceremonially "killed" before being put in the cache. With infinite patience, Mr. Willoughby succeeded in reconstructing the clay fragments into six recognizable figures, four men and two women. But only one of them was in good condition.

The battered figures stand upright or kneel. Their arms are held tightly against their sides and their legs

Left, a male figure, and right, kneeling man, both from the Turner Mound. *(Photos, Peabody Museum, Harvard University)*

are parallel to each other. One man holds his arms crossed over his chest in an attitude of reverence. Whatever the position, their shoulders are level, the heads face forward and the eyes look straight ahead. Their expressions are serious and solemn.

Despite the rigidly symmetrical design, the figures were done in a realistic style, like the animals on the effigy pipes. Proportions are lifelike and show an understanding of anatomical structure. The torsos and limbs of the standing and kneeling men were clearly defined. The fleshiness of the women was emphasized by the folds of fat that swell out above and below their tightly bound skirts. These figures were meant to be seen only from the front. Only the front of the body was rounded out and modeled, while the back was flattened and rendered simply. Perhaps the figures were meant to stand against the wall of a house.

Clay had a decided advantage for the artist because he could add a piece in one place or take some away in another until he had achieved the form he wanted. Unlike the hard stone, the more pliable clay could be squeezed, twisted, rolled, corrected and altered as often as the artist wanted. The body of the figure was first completely modeled, and then clothing, facial features and other details were individually fashioned and attached to the form.

The eyes are the most striking feature of the figures. They are shaped like raindrops and so sharply slanted that they give the figure an oriental expression. To add to the realism, the whites of the eyes were painted on the clay. The depressed foreheads conform to the common practice of head deformation. Nose, ears, curves of

Female figure, Turner Mound. *(Photo, Peabody Museum, Harvard University)*

the cheek, chin and the oval face are carefully and accurately modeled.

To judge from these figures, the men were tall and slender. The women were of a heavier, stockier build, which is not surprising in view of all the heavy work they were expected to perform in the village. They were all simply clothed because the climate in this region was mild the year round. The men wore a loincloth, the women a knee-length wraparound skirt. Incised lines on the surface indicate that moccasins were usually worn in the village. Some men had leggings, perhaps for long hunting or trading expeditions.

The artist made no attempt to glamorize or in any way to make his subjects more attractive. They are shown in everyday attire and wear few if any ornaments. The men and women seem to have stopped work momentarily and, in a somewhat self-conscious way, posed for the village artist. They combed their hair very simply; the women combed it back and tied it into a chignon, while the men tied their hair into one or more knots above their foreheads. None of them is represented as carrying any objects that might identify them as outstanding members of the community.

In 1945, under less dramatic circumstances, another group of figures was found in the Knight Mound on the Illinois River in southern Illinois. Fortunately they were well preserved and represent four women and one man. When the earth was brushed away, traces of color that had been painted on them still adhered to the clay. Although buried in a mound several hundred miles from where the Turner figures had been found, they have the same oval-shaped face, slanted eyes, full cheeks, prominent nose and lips, and the unemotional expression that is called Hopewell. They are several inches smaller than the Turner figures and different in style.

Unlike the Turner artist who sculpted realistically, the Knight Mound artist left out all unnecessary anatomical details and kept his figures quite simple. He did not worry about getting the proportions of the human body right any more than he tried to make faces like any particular person. The figures are dumpy and not in the least graceful or beautiful according to our standards.

The Knight figures do, however, show a variety of positions, unlike the stiffly posed Turner figures. The artist freed the arms from the body and also showed two

Seated woman, Knight Mound, Illinois. *(Photo, Illinois State Museum)*

mothers carrying their children. To fashion the arms, he probably rolled pieces of clay into strips, attached them to the body and quickly bent them in the middle to indicate the elbow. The fingers were merely a few incised lines. Even less care was given to the legs and feet. By pinching out the bottoms of the lumpy legs, feet of diminutive size were formed. The artist's lack of talent, or lack of concern for realism, is apparent in his attempt to show the seated position of two women. Instead of modeling the legs alongside the body, he merely outlined them in a mass beneath the figures. They wear the same clothing as the Turner figures, but the skirts are so tightly bound around the legs of the women that any movement would be impossible.

The head is the most important part of the figure. The artist exaggerated it so much that it is about one-third the size of the body. The facial features are somewhat broader and more crudely modeled. All figures have the same trait of a decided cleft in the upper lip. On three of the women, the hair cascades down the back to the waist, but one has it combed into a chignon like her Ohio cousin.

What the figures lacked in clothing, they more than made up for in colorful patterns and decorative accessories. All wear red ear spools which stand out vividly against their black hair. Shining beads or pearls are shown sewn on arm bands and moccasins and sometimes on the hems of the dresses. Skirts are painted black and decorated with red and white bands across the front. The most lavishly clothed woman, who may have been a dancer, wears an orange-belted skirt with a white bustle at the back. A many-strand necklace,

Three restored figures from the Knight Mound in Illinois. Top left, standing woman. Top right, seated man. Bottom left, woman carrying child. Bottom right, front view of woman carrying child. *(Photos, Illinois State Museum)*

white hair ribbons and decorative bracelets make her a very impressive figure. Before her she holds what some scholars claim to recognize as a turkey wing, but the shape is too vague to identify with certainty.

Most intriguing of all is the kneeling man whose body is wierdly painted in several contrasting colors. His white face gives him a ghostlike expression, emphasized by two red stripes that extend across his forehead to his eyes. His torso is purplish red, and running across his shoulder is a black, white and red band. The strange staff on which he rests his chin may be the source or symbol of his power. Whether he represented a priest,

Mother nursing child. *(Photo, Illinois State Museum)*

warrior, or other significant person is not known, but the elaborate body painting is most unusual and eerie.

Completely different in spirit are the two women shown with their children. The tender human feelings which they portray are rare in the art of primitive people. With considerable care the artist modeled the nursing child comfortably cradled in its mother's arms. The other child is shown carried on its mother's back. She holds its leg in one hand and reaches back with the other to grasp the child more securely. He tilts his head back, just as a child would do, in an attempt to see better what is going on. For some reason, the heads of these children are not as exaggerated in size and their body proportions are more realistic than those of the adults. They wear no clothes and probably ran naked most of the time. These two statues have a delightful charm, and they portray the universal love of mother for child which was as meaningful to these Indians 2,000 years ago as it is to us today.

The origin of the Knight figures seems to be as mysterious as the ideas they symbolize. Archaeologists were unprepared for their sudden appearance in a Hopewell mound in Illinois, a region where very little sculpture of any kind has been found. Some hint of their origin may be found in Mexico, which is believed to have been the source of corn cultivation, the practice of skull deformation and the style of the Adena pipe in the Ohio Valley.

It seems more than accidental that the Knight figures are strikingly like those made in the northwestern part of Mexico by Indian tribes known as the Tarascans. The Tarascan culture flourished at the same time as the

Two examples of figures of the Tarascan Culture, Mexico.

Hopewell. Not only did the Tarascan artists model their small figures in clay, they also did so in a style very much like that of the Knight figures. Women were the favorite subjects of the Tarascans, and they were often shown holding their children. The heads of the Mexican figures were similarly enlarged out of proportion, the eyes were given a decided slant and large ear spools were prominently displayed. The body was modeled with the same rubbery-type arms, lumpy legs and tiny feet. The Mexican women also wore only a skirt and loved to display a large necklace that covered most of their torso. Obviously the Tarascan and Knight figures are unusually similar in subject and style.

How this relationship between them can be accounted for is not clear. Whether or not the Hopewell Indians came in contact with the Tarascans while on extensive trading expeditions, or else the Mexicans traveled to the Ohio Valley for a short time, cannot be proven. Perhaps future research or excavation may turn up additional information to show how Mexican influence found its way into the culture of the Mound Builders.

8

Platform Pipes
and Smoking Tubes

INDIAN smokers in the ancient times of the Archaic,
Adena and Hopewell cultures had very different reasons for their use of tobacco from the cigarette smokers
of today. Both ancients and moderns may have found
the smoking habit a soothing one. But with the Indian
it early became associated with ritual and worship. Thus
it took on a sacred character which the Europeans and
later the Americans never shared, despite their mighty
consumption of the tobacco leaf.

Whatever the reason may have been — religious ritual or personal satisfaction — smoking spread rapidly
throughout the villages of the Adena and Hopewell Indians. Because hundreds of pipes have been found, some
scholars assume that the Indians may have grown tobacco in their garden plots along with squash, beans and
corn. Leaves of the cultivated tobacco plant are more
aromatic and milder than substitute herbs and wild
plants of the forest, and not so bitter. The Archaic In-

dians may have introduced the Mound Builders to the smoking habit, a theory based on discovery in their mounds of smoking tubes not unlike those of the Archaic peoples. But the Mound Builders improved upon the simple tube and sought to make it more elaborate.

The Adena carved their pipes with a straight-sided bowl near one end, and archaeologists call this the modified tubular pipe. One extraordinary Adena pipe was made by drilling the smoking tube through the sculptured figure of a standing Indian. Hopewell craftsmen designed their own special kind of smoking instrument, known as the platform pipe. Instead of carving a cylin-

Adena smoking pipes.

drical tube, they made a thin curved pedestal with a rounded bowl rising in the center. Modern archaeologists have sometimes called it the Monitor pipe because the design resembles that of the famous warship that defeated the *Merrimac* during the War Between the States. The platform pipe is the hallmark of the Hopewell culture. When Hopewell artists carved the bowls of these pipes in the shape of birds and animals, they transformed the mere smoking pipe into a work of sculpture unique in the history of art.

The platform pipe is about half the size of the Adena smoking tube, averaging between four and five inches

One example of a Hopewell platform pipe.

in length. While the larger Adena pipe may have needed the insertion of a narrower stem for comfortable smoking, the platform pipe was small and light enough to be held easily between the lips. Indian smokers did not carry the pipe clenched between their teeth as modern smokers often do. They held it in their hands and only put it to the mouth when inhaling. Rarely have teeth marks been found on these pipes.

The greatest number of platform pipes has been recovered from just two sites in southern Ohio: the Tremper Mound and Mound City. Sometimes the pipes had been placed in the graves with the dead; more often

Another Hopewell platform pipe.

they had been deposited in specially made caches on the mound floor. Almost 150 pipes were removed from a single cache in the Tremper Mound. Most of these had been deliberately broken, or *killed,* before being placed there by the Indians. Archaeologists worked painstakingly to restore them to their original shapes. These are the finest pipes ever made by the Hopewell Indians. Pipes found at other mound sites in Ohio and elsewhere are usually poor imitations. They are comparatively crude and clumsy in workmanship and do not display the high craftsmanship of the Tremper and Mound City pipes.

Unlike the Adena pipemakers who preferred limestone and sandstone for their pipes, the Hopewell artisans worked almost exclusively with pipestone. This is a very attractive stone and ideal for carving. It is soft, yet strong enough to resist splitting during the delicate cutting and drilling operations. To avoid the danger of breaking a finished pipe, the smoke channel was drilled while the pipe was still in a rough stage. Pipestone was eagerly sought because it is found in many colors and shades ranging from light gray to dark brown, and the surface of the stone is capable of taking a very high polish. Hopewell Indians discovered large deposits of this stone close at hand in the hills outside what is now Portsmouth. There one can still see the quarry pits once used by these prehistoric pipemakers.

While not as spectacular as the effigy bowl varieties, the plain pipes are in themselves very handsome. The slender platform is gently curved and the bowl is beautifully formed. A balanced sense of proportion also contributes to the beauty of the pipe. The carvers achieved this by making the bowl half the size of the platform. Even when the bowl, in some instances, was made high enough to extend above the eye level of the smoker, the platform was correspondingly lengthened so as to maintain the standard proportions. The highly polished surfaces enhance the charm and refinement of these plain pipes. They may antedate the more complex effigy pipes, but there is no way of knowing whether or not that is true.

The effigy bowl platform pipes are the best known carvings of Hopewell artists, and some examples rank among the finest sculpture made by primitive peoples anywhere in the world. The Indian artists lavished a wealth of imagination on these pipes which represented the animal kingdom around them. Although no larger than the palm of one's hand, these miniature figures are realistically shown in a variety of positions: standing, seated and crouching. The standard practice was to carve the bowl in the shoulder or back of the animal and join it with the smoke channel drilled through the interior of the platform. In almost all cases, the animal is so posed that it looks directly into the face of the smoker.

To make the eyes of these figures as realistic as possible, the artist often inserted a piece of copper or a freshwater pearl into holes carved for them. The smooth transparent material reflected light almost as a natural eye does. In other pipes, the eyes were simply incised on the surface. After the artist had completed all details of the carving, he smoothed and then highly polished

Flint clay platform effigy pipe representing hawk. Tremper Mound, Scioto County, Ohio. *(Courtesy of the American Museum of Natural History)*

the surface until all knife nicks and rough spots had been completely removed. The finished pipe was truly a work of art.

Realism is the great quality of these carvings and their lifelike creatures. Some threaten to fly away, like the Duck Hawk, poised to take flight and attack its prey; others seem ready to dash off the platform, like the otter proudly carrying a fish between its jaws. Sometimes the artists portrayed certain creatures in the act of seeking or devouring their food, like the raccoon with one foot in a crayfish hole, and the heron bending over to eat a fish that it caught with its long, pointed beak. To make these carvings even more true to life, the sculptor carefully showed the fish and the mud removed from the hole by the raccoon in low relief on the platforms. The Indian was a keen observer of nature, and he portrayed these creatures just as he saw them.

Despite the diversity of positions, the carvers were guided by a sense of symmetry. If a dividing line were drawn across the figure from one end of the platform to the other, the forms and details on one side would be almost identical to those on the other side. Often balanced symmetry makes stone sculpture seem static, unmoving. But the Hopewell artist had such a command

Platform effigy pipe representing otter with fish. Tremper Mound. *(Courtesy of the American Museum of Natural History)*

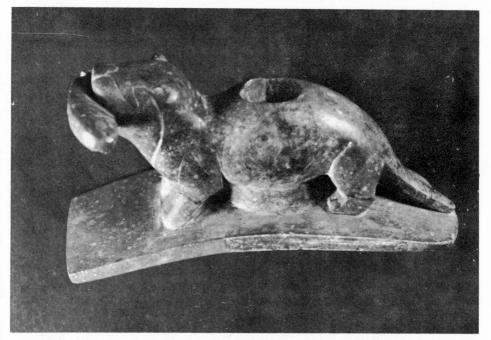

of his material and understanding of his subject that he imparted a sense of animation or potential movement to his carving. As he held the stone in one hand and chipped and gouged at it with primitive tools held in the other, the inanimate stone gradually grew into a recognizable creature endowed with the feeling of life.

A distinctive use of lines is another characteristic of Hopewell style, particularly in the bird carvings. With intricate and careful work, the artist even indicated the different feather markings: sawtooth patterns for the chest feathers, scale patterns for the light feathers on

Stone pipe, representing blue heron. Tremper Mound. *(Photo, Ohio State Museum)*

Stone frog pipe from Tremper Mound. *(Photo, Ohio State Museum)*

the leading edges of the wings, parallel lines to indicate folded wings and the tail of the bird. Even the texture of these feathers was expressed in line by varying the depth of the incisions. The artist dug more deeply into the stone to show heavier feathers, while wispy feathers were indicated with a lighter hand. A single, isolated line was used to distinguish between the lighter and darker colored feathers. In the Duck Hawk, for example, the undulating line that swings across the face and under the neck of the hawk indicates its distinctive dark moustache against the white background and hence makes its identification easy.

The delicate balance and sensitive modeling of these

creatures show how searching the artist's eye was, and how he emphasized those elements that best conveyed the character of his subject. The great power of the Duck Hawk was indicated in the broad shoulders and wings, thick muscular neck and sturdy legs. The hooked beak with which it tore at the flesh of its prey and the sharp talons used to catch its victims were clearly defined. Or consider the slim, sleek body of the otter, so magnificently portrayed that we can almost feel the underlying layer of fatty flesh that insulates him against the cold water. His head is broad and flat, and he looks out at the world through very small eyes. In proportion to his body his feet are short and stubby, a fact which discourages him from traveling overland although he can cover ground as fast as a man. His playful, frivolous nature must have attracted the attention of his Indian neighbors many times. Who but an otter spends so much time with his playmates tumbling and wrestling or paddling about in the river? The Indians also must have admired his ability as a fisherman and watched him stealthily creep up through the water to surprise many an unwary fish.

The frog was another favorite subject for the effigy pipes. He is shown on the platform just as he habitually rested on a lily pad or tree stump near the riverbank. The head is short and wide, the snout broadly circular. Despite his motionless attitude he is very much alive, and his tensely bent hind legs seem ready to propel him into the water at the first sign of danger. The artist shapes the broad body and short legs which give him a characteristic squat appearance. Just back of his head are two large kidney-shaped swellings, parotoid glands,

Hopewell smoking pipe representing duck seated on fish.

which secrete a milky substance used in his defense. A prominent bony ridge, called a cranial crest, is shown over and behind each eye.

One of the more imaginative Hopewell pipes shows a duck seated on a fish. The bowl was made in the back of the duck, and the smoke was drawn through an opening in the mouth of the fish. The eyes of both creatures were originally inlaid with pearls, but these have long since fallen out and become lost. This pipe was modeled from clay instead of stone and hardened by subjecting it to the intense heat of fire. But fired clay is not as strong as stone, and at some point the bill of the duck broke off. It was ingeniously repaired by Indian craftsmen who made holes in the head and bill at the point of the break. A copper dowel was inserted in the holes, and the two pieces were fitted together. The fit was so perfect that the break is almost imperceptible even today. Several other stone pipes had also been repaired in this way with dowels.

How could the Hopewell artist have gained the knowledge necessary to depict these fleet-footed and high-flying creatures with such accuracy on smoking pipes? The hunter may have brought him the wild game that he had killed. Some animals and birds, among them the otter, duck and frog, may have been captured in snares and traps and kept in wooden cages and raised for food. More friendly animals may have been trained and kept as pets. In either case, the artist would have had a chance to study his subjects. More elusive creatures, however, could only be studied in their natural habitat. The accuracy of the physical details suggests that the artist first made sketches, perhaps on a sheet of birch bark, which helped guide him in his sculpture. While we can only guess at his method, we must marvel at his results. The effigy pipes provide us with a zoological picture collection of the bird and animal life that inhabited the Ohio Valley more than 2,000 years ago. Together, these carvings rival the encyclopedic collection of birds and animals painted by John James Audubon during the last century.

Several pipes found in one mound at Mound City are in the shape of human heads. Like the animal pipes, they had been purposely broken before burial. When reassembled they, too, were found to face the smoker. These are serious, unsmiling faces and look out with large and open yet sightless eyes. Perhaps they were carved after the deaths of the important people buried in the mound. The artist portrayed the fleshy and bony structure of the features with studied realism. The

Stone pipe representing male head, from Mound City, Ohio. *(Photo, Ohio State Museum)*

outer margin of the ear was perforated with a series of holes that originally may have been inlaid with copper or pearls as a sign of beauty or social status. While we cannot be sure whom they represent, there is no doubt that the elaborately decorated individuals must have been chieftains, priests or great warriors. What other explanation is there for the incised lines across the face from forehead to chin? They may indicate tattooing or painting, as both were practiced by ancient Indian tribes. A grand headdress emphasizes the importance of one. The border is decorated with a row of inlaid pearls, and two horns project from the sides. Whatever the reason for their existence, these pipes are rare examples of Hopewell effigy pipes.

Shrouded in mystery and the subject of considerable controversy is the one human figure carved in the form of a smoking pipe. It was found sixty years ago near the outstretched hand of an Indian brave who had been buried in the famous Adena Mound from which the culture derives its name. When and where it was carved and whom it represents are questions that still remain to be answered. Not only is this the only carving of a human figure known to have been made by the Adena, it is also unlike the style of any Hopewell figures. It is unique in the art of the Mound Builders.

The pipe was modeled from a hard-fired clay and is a soft yellow color in front and brick red at the back. Essentially it is shaped like a smoking tube, with the mouthpiece above the head and the tobacco chamber between the legs. The smoke channel is hollowed out

Stone pipe representing raccoon, from Tremper Mound. *(Photo, Ohio State Museum)*

through the interior of the figure and gradually increases in width as it approaches the base. The upper part of the figure is modeled in three dimensions, while the legs are carved in high relief around the tube. Three incisions on the torso, arranged like an arrow point, represent the stomach structure and rib cage. The surface of the figure is very highly polished.

The figure is carved with a breechcloth, decorated with a feathered bustle at the rear and incised serpentine design on the front. The design resembles the one incised on bone by an Indian of the Archaic period. Perhaps this was a well-known design, and the Adena artist merely borrowed it. The hair is more like that of an Algonkian Indian than of an ancient Hopewellian. It was apparently cut close to the side of the head, leaving a cockscomb at the top. This was parted in the center and combed to either side. The texture of the hair is indicated by finely incised lines on the surface. The lobes of the ears are enormously distended by hollow plugs, a practice common to many primitive people as a sign of beauty. This was usually accomplished in the following way. When the Indian was a small child, holes were made in the earlobes and a small plug inserted. As the years passed, the hole was enlarged gradually by larger and larger plugs and the flesh stretched just as if it were rubber. Plugs even larger than the ones worn by the Adena Indians have been observed among other primitive peoples.

The enlarged head of the effigy, the bent knees, the arms tightly held along the sides give it an extraordinary intensity. Because of its chunky proportions, emphasis on musculature of limbs, deeply undercut facial features and the four-sided blocklike character of the carving as a whole, it recalls the style of certain examples of ancient Mexican sculpture. Some scholars believe that the Adena artist was somehow acquainted with Mexican art, although no examples like this effigy pipe have ever been found south of the Rio Grande.

While some researchers seek the origin of its style, others are more interested in whom the carving represents. There is some justification for the belief shared by a number of scholars that it represents a dwarf. They have pointed out that the proportions of the figure conform to specific characteristics of a dwarf: enlarged head set on a muscular body of normal proportions, with stubby arms and legs. Other scholars believe that no dwarf was intended, but rather that the disproportionately large head is characteristic of primitive art throughout the world. The head is the most distinctive and significant part of a human being, and consequently many primitive artists believe it should be given more emphasis. If we are to interpret this carving as a realistic portrait, then the swollen neck might also reveal a goiter condition, and the enlarged limb joints might be symptoms of rachitis, a disease of the skeletal system. Because of their abnormalities, dwarfs and other deformed people were often accorded much respect by their tribes. One dwarf was given an elaborate burial in an Adena Mound in Kentucky.

Thus archaeology has uncovered for us one Adena Indian who stands today behind the glass pane of a museum case, his birth and history lost in the ancient past.

9

The Hawk and the Artist

THE Duck Hawk flew high over the mounds and villages of the prehistoric American Indians, his slender tail and long pointed wings silhouetted against the blue sky. To the Indians watching below, the bird symbolized the strength and striking power of a mighty hunter. Soaring calmly across the heavens, the hawk would suddenly wheel and dive at some prey below with amazing velocity, like a streak of lightning. Whether he struck a blow or grasped his prey, the Duck Hawk killed instantaneously. He was the mortal enemy of small creatures of the sky such as pigeons, sparrows, robins and bluejays as well as fowl, and small mammals like mice and moles. With his prey securely clutched in his mighty talons, he returned to his craggy home high in the hills. From these heights the hawk surveyed the waters and valley below. He was master of the sky, where he reigned.

This is why the hawk captured the imagination of these ancient Indians. Living out-of-doors as they did, they had many opportunities to admire the speed and effective hunting tactics of this fearless fighter. Although we popularly call him the Duck Hawk, he is the Peregrine Falcon, whose European cousin was the famous Hunting Falcon immortalized in the song and poetry of the Middle Ages. His body is small, averaging about one and a half feet, but his wing span measures slightly under four feet. Almost forty different species of hawks are known in North America, but the Duck Hawk is the most ferocious member of the family and perhaps the fiercest and swiftest bird of prey known to man.

Of all the birds and animals, he best symbolized the prowess of hunting required of the Indian brave. Just as he was deified by the ancient Egyptians more than 4,000 years ago, so he may have been glorified by the mound-building Indians. Certainly his presence was immortalized in many magnificent carvings.

The hawk was not the only creature portrayed in the art of these Indians. There were other birds, such as the crow and the owl, and a variety of animals, among them dogs, frogs, squirrels and otters. On only a few occasions did the artists carve statues of their fellow villagers. These human figures make up no more than a small fraction of the total sculpture uncovered by archaeologists. It was the bird and animal kingdom that appealed to these Indian artists.

How did these creatures appear in the eyes of the artist? Very often they were carved in a remarkably lifelike style, and because of this realism are easy to identify. Less often the artist portrayed his subject in a more abstract style. For example, in carving the hawk he did not include all its physical details; he defined only the outstanding characteristics of prominent hooked beak, large eyes and sharp-pointed talons. Sometimes his carving became so abstract that the subject cannot be identified. The art of these Indians progressed through all the stages from realism to abstraction.

The different materials imposed different styles upon the primitive artists. In one way or another they used every natural material at hand. Stone was the preferred medium, but wonderful carvings were also made of copper, mica, shell and bone. The Indians achieved these results with only the simplest tools and a considerable amount of labor. To the Indian, time was unimportant; it was the beauty of the finished object that counted.

The consistently high quality of the art indicates that not everyone was an artist; it was probably the work of specialists who enjoyed a training as thorough and profound as any formal learning gained in an art academy today. Perhaps the profession of Indian artists was hereditary and skills were passed down from father to son. This would account for the uniform craftsmanship. Judging by other Indian tribes, men were the sculptors and women the weavers and pottery makers. These artists were indeed experts, and their work was highly prized by the villages in which they worked. In return for his art, the craftsman may have been supported by his fellow tribesmen who brought him food and other necessities of life.

How can the consistently high quality of Hopewell sculpture be explained? Obviously, great artists like these Indians did not develop overnight. Any artist must undergo many years of study and practice before he can produce his finest work. His first works are generally hesitant and even fumbling attempts. Yet strangely, archaeologists have never found a single crude carving that would illustrate the early development period of the artist. Just as art critics judge sculpture today, perhaps there were certain Indians of refined taste who examined all the carvings and accepted only the better ones. If such were the case, then the rejected pieces may have been destroyed, and this would explain why no trace of them has been found.

Most of the Hopewell carvings are unique, none like them having been found anywhere in the world. Some carvings are reminiscent of the techniques and styles of the birdstones made by the Archaic Indians. This is not surprising in view of the fact that some members of the Hopewell community may have been descendants of the Archaic people, lived in the same region and retained a number of the traits of their predecessors. Many Adena carvings, however, seem more related to the art of the ancient Mexican Indians. Some scholars point out that the Adena may also have introduced into the Ohio Valley the cultivation of maize and the practice of skull deformation common to peoples south of the Rio Grande. Whether or not the Adena once lived in or near the region of Mexico and brought these southern customs with them when they migrated is a question that still remains unanswered.

Because these beautiful carvings came from Adena and Hopewell mounds in the Ohio Valley, we may indeed consider that the first art academy in what is now the United States was founded here more than 2,000 years ago, and that the Duck Hawk was the favorite model of the artists.

10

Variations on a Theme

BEFORE discussing the carvings of the Duck Hawk, let us consider for a moment the matter of terminology. Realism, abstractionism and symbolism are some of the terms frequently used to describe the different styles of Hopewell and Adena art. These words are also used to describe works of art today. What do these *isms* mean?

Realism refers to those carvings which were done from life and hence are true to nature. The first efforts of the Indian artist who lived in the wild were realistic. His survival depended upon his acute vision and understanding of the life and habits of the animals which he stalked for food or avoided out of fear. Because he thought so much about these creatures, it is not surprising to find that many of his carvings are extraordinarily lifelike or realistic.

Many other carvings of the hawk are abstract in style. The artist gradually abandoned a realistic representation and reduced the figure of the hawk to a few essential lines. He worked from memory instead of from life, and in doing so he disregarded many of the features and accentuated only those that he considered important — toothed beak, large circular eyes, curved talons and wavy lines of the wing and tail. Of these five features, the head with its prominent beak and eye was the most commonly shown. Other parts of the body were so highly abstracted in shape as to prevent identification.

When the hawk was reduced to a simple basic shape used over and over again in the art of the Hopewell and Adena Indians, it became stylized or conventionalized. Such a form then became a symbol. Even if the form became so abstract as to almost defy identification, it nevertheless was a symbol of the hawk. Thus the real-

DUCK HAWK

DETAIL

DETAIL

DETAIL

DETAIL
MEXICAN STAMP SEAL

DETAIL

DETAIL

VARIATIONS OF DUCK HAWK

istic representation of the hawk was eventually replaced by symbolism, where a few characteristic traits sufficed to convey the idea or spirit of the bird. Regardless of how conventionalized or complex the symbolism of the hawk, its presence must have been recognized in the art by all the villagers. The use of symbols to convey the idea of a subject has been used the world over by primitive artists, and it can also be recognized in the works of a growing number of modern artists.

Whether realistic or abstract, all carvings were executed with a strong sense of symmetry and rhythm. That symmetry played such an important role in the artist's thinking is not surprising, since almost all the things he saw were symmetrically constructed, among them leaves and flowers, open clamshells, skeletons and skins of hunted animals and human beings. Because all living things are created according to an underlying symmetrical law, it is not strange to find this feeling for symmetry in the artist's creation. Rhythm or movement is another characteristic of the natural world, and it can also be recognized in his art. Moving clouds, rippling rivers, running animals, flying birds, gusts of winds; the phenomena of the natural world that inspired in the sensitive Indian artist the feeling for rhythm and movement are endless.

Hopewell and Adena Indians, like other primitive peoples, evidently accepted abstract art and its artists perhaps more generally and generously than such are accepted today. Many of the most highly valued carvings that have been found in excavations of their burial mounds can be classified as abstract art. These carvings stood the test of sophisticated art critics when exhibited not too long ago in the Museum of Modern Art in New York City.

It is a fascinating experience to trace the evolution of the hawk throughout the art of the Mound Builders. In place of painting, which was of little interest to these Indians, the image of the hawk appeared on such different materials as copper, bone, stone and the surface of clay pottery. Between the two extremes of realism and abstraction, stylistic variations of the figure of the hawk were many. There were divergent art traditions in the work of Indians 2,000 years ago just as there are in the work of artists today.

Copper duck hawk, Mound City, Ohio. *(Photo, Ohio State Museum)*

The most realistic example of the Duck Hawk was cut out of sheet copper and placed in a grave in one of the mounds at the Mound City group. The artist clearly recorded his impression of the hawk in flight, apparently bent on attacking its prey. He carefully outlined the full body of the hawk with its powerful wing, broad tail, toothed beak and large eye. The artist even indicated the distinctive *moustache* marking of the species with an undulating line that curves across the face. Like the artist who carved the hawk from stone in the form of a smoking pipe, he used different markings and patterns to indicate various types of feathers and their textures.

This is a magnificent copper carving. The artist certainly depicted the spirited flight of the hawk with vitality and accuracy. The more is the wonder, since the artist worked only with the crudest of equipment. The edges are finely cut, as if made with shears, whereas the Indians had only stone or copper knives. These were used as effectively as modern machine-made tools.

Abstraction, rather than realistic depiction of the hawk, seemed more important to other Indian artists. Instead of attempting an exact copy of nature, they selected only certain features characteristic of the hawk and conventionalized these into a decorative style.

This variation from realism is evident in two examples from the Mound City group: one incised on a copper tablet and the other cut out of the same metal. Obviously they are related in form and style. In each case the heads of two hawks are portrayed facing away from each other. The artist focused his attention upon the gently curved shape of the head and larged-toothed beak. No attempt was made to reproduce other parts of the bird's structure. The bodies were abstracted into simple rounded elements and cleverly joined together. The graceful rounded shapes, clear incisive lines and strict symmetry of composition belong perfectly to Hopewell art.

How could the artist have achieved such perfect sym-

Duck hawk (engraved copper), Mound City. *(Photo, Ohio State Museum)*

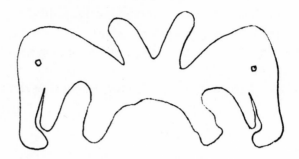

Still another engraved copper duck hawk, Mound City.
(Photo, Ohio State Museum)

metry with two hawks? It seems to be true, as some
scholars believe, that a stencil may have been made by
the artist for just this purpose. An Indian could certainly make a stencil as easily as children do in class-
rooms today. Instead of paper, however, he may have
used a thin sheet of birch bark, folded it and with a
sharp knife cut out half of his design from the edge
towards the crease. When the bark stencil was opened,
the cutout pattern would be repeated in two identical
designs. Because of the amazing symmetry of the designs, the artist may have perfected this or some other
kind of mechanical aid to help him achieve the balance
that he desired.

Similar in design is the image of the hawk on a pottery vessel found hundreds of miles to the south of Ohio
in a Hopewell mound in Louisiana. The head of the
hawk is just like those represented on copper, but the
body seems charged with energy and threatens to wrig-
gle off the vessel. The artist increased the vividness of

144

Hopewell pottery at left, and, below, detail of the design. *(Photo, Smithsonian Institution)*

Two hawks cut out of copper, Mound City.

the hawk by roughening the surrounding background
area. This design must have been made immediately
after the vessel had been formed and while the clay was
still soft and damp. The design became indelible only
after the vessel was baked and hardened. The upper
part of the vessel was decorated with floral shapes like
leaves and vines. These motifs were not unusual because
this region was heavily forested, as much of it still is
today.

Even more abstract in style is the design of the hawk
from the Hopewell Mound group cut from another sheet
of copper. At first glance, the hawk is almost unidenti-
fiable. But it is possible to recognize the familiar conventional pattern of large beak and eye of two hawks
facing away from each other, as in other examples from
Mound City. Once again, the body is represented by
simple rounded elements, and the design as a whole is
governed by a strict symmetry.

An interesting variation is the figure of the hawk portrayed at both ends of a carefully shaped piece of animal bone found at the Hopewell Mound group. Here the elongated beak merges into the edge of the bone, while the wings consist of two graceful strips. The clarity of the hawk image was emphasized by roughening the background, as on the pottery vessel. The space at each end of the bone was filled with five sharply defined shapes of grizzly-bear canine teeth which add to the attractiveness of the design.

Hawk engraved on bone. Seip Mound, Ohio. *(Photo, Ohio State Museum)*

BERLIN TABLET
ADENA, OHIO

FLORENCE TABLET
ADENA, OHIO

WRIGHT TABLET
ADENA, KENTUCKY

These several representative examples show how the Hopewell artist delighted in executing variations on the theme of the hawk. He was not always interested in realism, because he was not trying to reproduce nature exactly. What interested him most was distorting the hawk design into interesting shapes and patterns.

The Adena artist represented the hawk in a style and technique different from that of the Hopewell. Instead of using copper, he portrayed the image of the hawk on small stone tablets cut into rectangular and oval shapes. Sometimes the design was engraved into the surface of the stone with a sharp, pointed tool, at other times the background was scraped away and the design itself left standing in very low relief. Of the twelve tablets known to have been made by Adena artists, most represent the hawk, but in more complex and intriguing designs than in the Hopewell art. Although related to each other, slight variations occur among them, and seldom are the designs dull or uninspired. For the sake of convenience, archaeologists refer to these tablets by name, names based on the specific mounds or places where the tablets were found. These tablet designs are truly characteristic of Adena art. Although limited in quantity, most of them are outstanding in quality and make a celebrated contribution to American Indian art.

One version of the hawk which is easily identifiable shows the bird flattened in profile against the stone. In this so-called Berlin tablet, found almost a century ago in a mound near Berlin, Ohio, there are the familiar beak, large eye (now strangely decorated with an H-shaped motif), and the sinuous body curved and compressed upon itself almost like a serpent. The rhyth-

149

mic movement of this figure is more like that of the hawk portrayed on the Hopewell vessel from Louisiana than examples found in other Ohio mounds. Beneath the body, completely filling the space, are the legs and talons shown one in front of the other. The wing is a simple rounded shape marked with a scalloped border. The design is more linear in style and complicated in composition than any of the examples of Hopewell art.

Not very different from the Berlin tablet is the design engraved on the surface of a small bone disk that had originally been removed from the upper part of a human skull. The head, wing and talons of the hawk seem to have been dismembered and reassembled by the artist so that they swarm across the surface of the bone. Museum authorities have darkened the surrounding area so that the design stands out clearly. Related to it in style is the design on the Wright tablet. The hawk is similarly portrayed, but in low relief. Unfortunately, the tablet has been broken and much of the design is lost. The scallop-edged shape beneath the body recalls the symbol of the wing on the Berlin tablet.

These three designs are related in style and not difficult to identify. Other examples, however, are far more complicated and abstract in form.

Engravings on the Wilmington and Meigs tablets portrayed the hawk in complex designs. Of the two, the Wilmington design is superior in style and technique. The artist tried to arrange his geometric shapes in such a way that they were combined into a balanced unit. Although the design was highly abstract, there was an underlying symmetry and order in the composition. He placed two confronting hawks at the top of

Adena engraved tablet of stone, Wilmington, Ohio. *(Courtesy, Ohio State Museum)*

the design, but tried to represent the faces by flattening them and placing one eye directly above the other, as in a Picasso portrait. The necks and chests are a series of lines that run down the center of the design and join near the base of the tablet. The tails, reduced to sev-

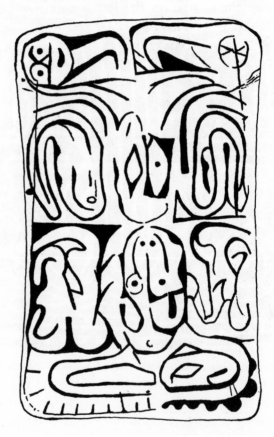

Adena engraved tablet of stone, Meigs. *(Courtesy, Heye Foundation)*

eral wavy lines, fill the lower part of the design. The left and right sides of the composition have been divided into four equal-size sections and each section filled with drastically abstracted wings and talons, placed one above the other. These parts are curved, bent and twisted in shape. Abstraction and near abstraction of the physical structure of the hawk are the chief elements of the design.

The Wilmington tablet was carved in two different techniques: the design on the left is in low relief while the design on the right was engraved into the surface of the stone. The Meigs tablet is cruder in technique, and its design differs slightly from that of the Wilmington. This is seen in the addition of two oval-shaped patterns, possibly representing wings, in the center of the design.

On first sight, these designs seem strange and even baffling. The fantastic treatment of the hawk by the rich, imaginative mind of the Indian artist may seem far removed from our classical concept of sculpture. But the creative, well-ordered, magnificently carved design on the Wilmington tablet stands as one of the most attractive examples of American Indian art.

Abstraction is carried to the extreme in the Cincinnati tablet found in 1841 in a mound outside of Cincinnati. In plan it is symmetrically divided into balanced sections like the Meigs tablet, but specific features of the hawk are not evident. Because the shapes with the two large patterns at the top resemble the curved beak and eye, this tablet has been included in the hawk category. Obviously it is a decoration. The motifs are of a sort that seem to have been derived

Adena engraved stone tablet, Cincinnati. *(Courtesy, Ohio State Museum)*

from several features of the hawk, but strictly rendered in abstract pattern. Attempts to discover recognizable forms in this geometry of pattern are thwarted. The original meaning of the total design has long since been lost.

For a full appreciation of the Cincinnati tablet, one must forget realistic portrayal and appreciate the design as a decorative scheme in itself, as in many modern paintings. The artist had an instinct for pattern and took every opportunity to spread a rich design across the surface of the tablet. The design is highly decorative, the craftsmanship is superb and the object lastingly appealing. This striking engraving ranks as one of the finest examples of abstract art.

Nobody knows why these tablets were carved. Since they have been found in graves, one theory might be that they were made exclusively for the dead. Unlike the Hopewell objects, these had no holes drilled in them to be strung and worn. Traces of red paint on the surface of two tablets suggest that they were used as stamps. The surface of the design might have been covered with paint, and while the color was still wet, the tablet pressed against the skin or clothing. When removed, a vivid colored impression of the design would remain. Perhaps the chieftains or medicine men decorated themselves this way.

Similarly made tablets are known to have been used this way by some of the ancient Mexican cultures. Because these Mexican stamps were made of clay and were small enough to be carried easily, they were widely traded, and some of them may have reached the Ohio Valley. That they may have been seen by the Hopewell and Adena Indians is strongly suggested by the fact that some of the Mexican stamps also depicted a bird of prey, like the hawk, and in a style not far removed from that of the Mound Builders. Until archaeologists can piece together more of the puzzle of cultural relationships between these two distant regions, it is all a matter of conjecture.

Another question is posed by the presence of grooves on the backs of some tablets. These seem to have been made by the sharpening of a tool. Possibly the artist himself made them while keeping a sharp point on his engraving tool. Some authorities believe that these tablets were the prized possessions of medicine men. During certain blood-letting rituals, not uncommon to Indian tribes, the medicine man may have sharpened the point of his knife on the tablet before piercing the flesh of his victim. Lurid descriptions of such human sacrifice have come down to us from the accounts of the early Spanish conquistadores in Central Mexico and Yucatan.

Whatever the origin and meaning of the hawk designs, these Adena engravings are of a high quality workmanship. Looking at them after a lapse of 2,000 years, it seems difficult to deny their makers the title of artists.

Duck hawk stamp seal, Mexico.

11

Rivals of the Hawk

MANY creatures vied with the Duck Hawk for the Hopewell artist's attention — birds, mammals, fish, reptiles and human figures. These subjects, however, were only occasionally portrayed, in contrast with the artist's preoccupation with the hawk. Besides living forms, a rich variety of abstract motifs was also present in their art. While some abstractions seem to have been derived from plant forms, others were purely geometric. Practically every available material was enhanced with engraved designs or else cut into handsome abstract shapes. All carvings customarily were small and either perforated with small holes or, as in the case of animal and human bones, hollowed out so as to permit them to be strung and worn. Embellishment was often the purpose of this scultpure, but some carvings apparently were created for ritual or ceremonial needs.

One of the highly symbolic designs was engraved on both sides of a piece of parietal bone taken from a hu-

Stone human effigy pipe, Adena Mound *(Photo, Ohio State Museum)*

man skull. The Indians had deliberately broken the carving before depositing it in a ceremonial cache of the Turner Mound, but except for a few missing pieces it has been perfectly restored by archaeologists. The designs on both sides of the bone are identical in the basic essentials. In the center of the design is a wierd, cat-like creature. Its head is shown as a circle with large pointed eyes, while its front legs dangle below, the

Cat and hawk engraved on section of parietal bone, Turner Mound

Left, human face engraved on section of human bone, Hopewell Mound group. At right, opened line representation of same section of bone. *(Photo, Chicago Museum)*

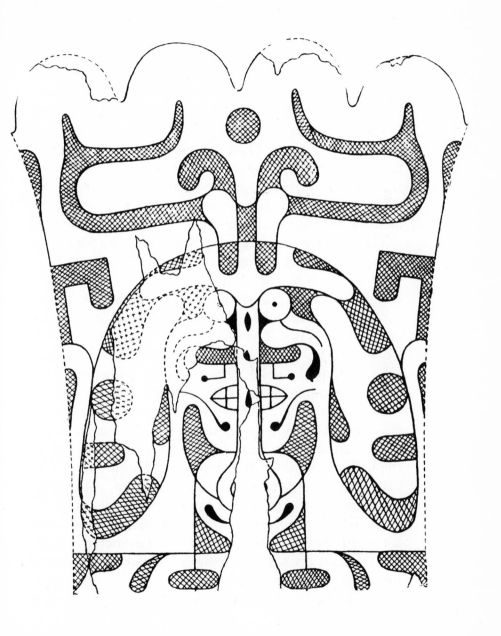

claws menacingly extended. The creature has been so highly abstracted that its body is nonexistent, but the presence of the body is nevertheless implied. Curved shapes with crosshatched lines contribute to the complexity of the design. Perhaps these were meant to represent the striped fur markings on this mysterious cat.

But the cat is not alone. The large circular eye and toothed beak of the Duck Hawk, placed in a reversed position, can be recognized on the right side of the design. At the opposite side is another dotted eye, identical in shape, that may represent another creature whose identity cannot be determined.

This is truly an extraordinary design. The forms are so strange that we can only wonder what they may have symbolized to the mind of these Indians. Perhaps the design represented a mythical creature that combined the prowess and killing instincts of the cat with those of the Duck Hawk. The carving may have been an amulet, or charm, worn by a great Hopewell hunter, and the fact that the design was engraved on human bone may have enhanced its magic power.

Such combinations of the real with the fantastic are also seen in the intriguing image of a human face engraved around a piece of human bone found in one of the larger mounds of the Hopewell Mound group. The effigy, like the symbol of death, wears an antler-horn headdress which identifies it as that of a Hopewell chieftain. His face is distorted into a hideous grimace, and his tightly clenched teeth are bared. Geometric motifs, like those on the cat engraving, are scattered across the surface of the design.

Archaeologists do not know why the artist made such

an unusual design or what it meant. More than likely it was the funerary image of a dead chieftain. How better to reveal the spirit of the dead than by abstracting the face into a fantastic other-worldly image of death? This is one of the unique Hopewell carvings that illustrate a concern with death and terror. Such representations usually seem to have been avoided by the Hopewell artists.

The origin of the antler-horn headdress presents another interesting question. This distinctive headdress has been found sporadically in the Mound Building area, beginning with the Archaic people. It has a far older history in Europe and Asia. The earliest appearance of the antler-horn headdress was in a painting made on the walls of a cave in France during the Ice Age about 20,000 years ago. It was worn by a strangely masked dancing figure presumably performing a ceremonial rite. Scholars have since traced this ceremonial headdress eastward and found it to have been particularly widely used among many nomadic peoples who roamed throughout the vast region of Siberia after the Ice Age. Because of the proximity of northeastern Asia to America, some scientists believe the antler-horn headdress may have been brought across the Bering Strait by some of the early migrants.

There is also the possibility, however, that the antler-horn headdress may have been created by the mound-building Indians, independently of any other culture. It may have been part of a disguise worn by hunters when stalking deer. Whatever the origin of the headdress, there is no question that with the passing of time it became increasingly common among many Indian tribes and played an important role in their religious ceremonies.

Aside from this engraving, carvings of human forms were seldom found, despite the many works turned out by the Hopewell artists. Rare examples of their appearance are, therefore, of great interest, particularly the few figurines cut out of copper and mica and found in graves of the Hopewell Mound group and Mound City. Regardless of where they were found, or the material from which they were shaped, they are all essentially the same. They stand with legs bent at the knees, feet pointing outwards and arms attached to the bodies, except where they had been broken off above the elbows. All these forms are headless — mere silhouettes of human beings, nameless shadows out of a distant past. Tiny holes along the upper edge of the neck indicate they were meant to be sewn on garments; or perhaps the missing parts were fashioned separately and attached to the form as one would assemble a doll. But such individual parts have not yet been found.

Stylistically, these standing figures reveal a close affinity to the clay figures from the Turner Mound. The proportions are identical, and they were carved with the same feeling for full-bodied, rounded limbs. But the question of why they were carved and whom they represent still remains unanswered.

An extremely sensitive carving found at the Seip Mound portrays the trumpeter swan, skillfully cut out of a fragile piece of tortoise shell. The artist conventionalized the figure into a few simple elements that expressed the grace, rhythm and beauty of form so characteristic of this majestic bird. He carved the swan just

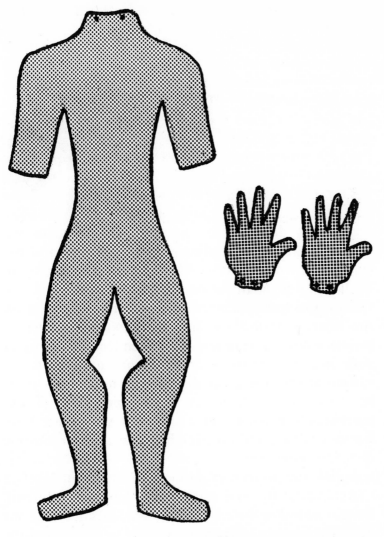

Above, copper representation of human hands, Mound City. Left, standing human figure of **mica** from Hopewell Mound group.

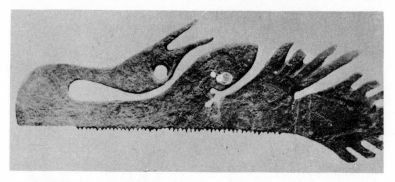

Trumpeter swan of shell, Seip **Mound.**

as he had often seen it gliding across the waters of the
Ohio River with its neck curled back as if struggling to
swallow a fish caught in its sharp beak.

This is a splendid white bird and the largest of all
American waterfowl. It averages about five feet in
length and has a wing span up to ten feet. It can fly at
great heights, and its resonant discordant trumpetings
can be heard over great distances. The Indians must
have marveled at the beauty of its flight, wings glisten-
ing like silver against blue sky, and they must have
watched with bated breath when it swam considerable
distances under water.

Today the trumpeter swan is nearly extinct. After
the arrival of the first settlers, the bird was wantonly
slaughtered. Its flesh served as food, its feathers for
decorative apparel. Its nests were also invaded, and the
eggs and helpless young taken as prized delicacies for
the dinner table. That the Hopewell artist knew and
admired the trumpeter swan is indicated in the beauty

166

of this design which expresses the charming essence of the creature and is so perfectly suited to the beauty of the shell material.

More realistic in style are several identical carvings of the sucker fish, a member of the carp family, cut out of sheet copper and found together in one of the mounds at Mound City. The species is easily identified because of the artist's accurate portrayal of its broad fleshy mouth with which it sucks up aquatic plants and animals. This is a particularly sluggish fish that feeds along the river bottoms and may attain a considerable size, sometimes reaching a length of three feet and weighing up to ten or more pounds. Although its flesh is bony and has a distinctive muddy taste, it is nevertheless edible and may have been an important staple of the Hopewell diet. The realistic style of the fish coupled with the perforations made in its body suggest that it was worn as an amulet, perhaps to insure a good catch of fish.

A number of curious carvings have been recovered

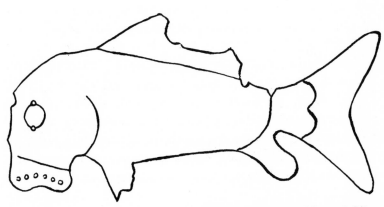

Copper fish from Mound City.

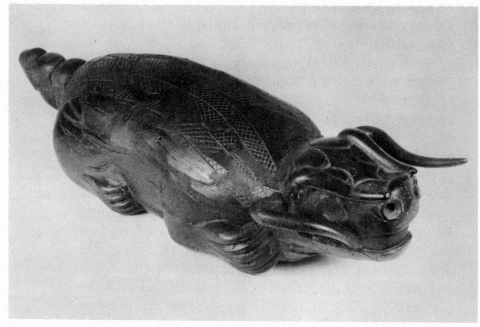

Horned monster of slate from Turner Mound. *(Photo, Peabody Museum, Harvard University)*

from the Turner Mound, including the engraved image of the cat. Two equally symbolic works from the same mound are the horned serpent cut out of mica and a strange horned monster carved from red slate. Both carvings had been broken by the Indians before placement in the ceremonial cache, and only through the extraordinary patience of archaeologists have they been restored to their original state. In style and spirit these carvings suggest a relationship to the art of ancient Mexico. Other hints of Mexican influence have been reported from the Turner Mound, particularly the presence of maize common to Indians south of the Rio

Grande. But again, until more specific evidence is uncovered, archaeologists can do no more than speculate about these unusual features of the Turner Mound.

The horned serpent, with its massive head, notched tail and tensely coiled body, resembles the rattlesnake. Just as with the portrayal of the rattlesnake in ancient Mexican art, the horns or plumes are indicated with incised lines that extend across the snake's head. That the two holes in the eye socket were meant to hold a freshwater pearl was proven to be true when the archaeologist luckily found the now blackened pearl mixed in with the ashes of the ceremonial cache. Before it was broken and buried in the mound, the silvery mica body and eye of lustrous white pearl must have made this serpent look like a supernatural spirit from another world.

The enormous Serpent Mound nearby shows that the snake played an important role in the religious beliefs of these people. Perhaps the serpent symbolized a protective spirit, or the heavens, as it did among other Indian tribes. Perhaps it symbolized eternal life because of the snake's annual habit of shedding its skin and thereby seeming to renew its life. The fact that this mica serpent was placed together with the clay figurines leads to the belief that it may have symbolized life in another world. The serpent, strangely enough, was rarely carved by Hopewell artists, although the Serpent Mound was the greatest monument of all.

The meaning of the horned monster is a baffling question. This creature has the body of a quadruped and the head and horns of a serpent. The notched tail also resembles the rattles of the rattlesnake. Its unusual short,

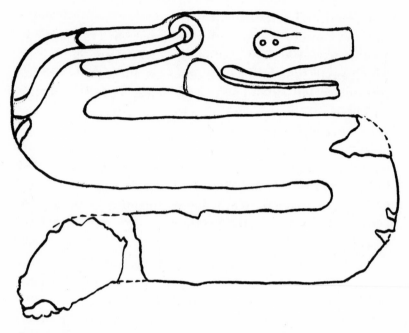

Serpent in mica from Turner Mound (restored).

heavy legs are attached to the body with claws, shown by incised lines. Across the back of its shell are two bands filled with crosshatched lines that contribute to its unusual appearance. The head of the beast reveals its ferocious nature. The long horns had been inserted into holes specially drilled for them. The holes of the eyes were probably filled with pearls, and two holes drilled into the upper and lower jaws may have been inlaid with pointed teeth. Its mouth is partly open, and the artist clearly indicated its large sharp teeth with incised lines. The interior of the stone was hollowed out as if the carving were meant to be attached to a wooden staff and carried about the village.

Although the creature cannot be identified, legends of several Indian tribes of North America vividly describe a water monster which they regarded as a mythical being of the other world. There is no way of knowing whether or not.this Hopewell carving portrays this specific creature.

In the designs derived from plant life or those purely geometric in character, three specific motifs prevail throughout: tightly bent comma shapes, graceful rounded scrolls and circles, usually dotted. Often the circles are enclosed within the scrolls and form a compact pattern. Using these repeated motifs, the artists

Engraved designs on steatite stones, Hopewell.

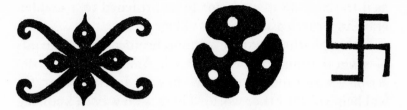

Copper designs, Hopewell.

created highly original and decorative patterns. The variety of designs based on combinations of these motifs is endless, yet all are unmistakably Hopewell in style. They are pleasing in shape and proportion, executed with a curvilinear sweeping quality and governed by a strong sense of balance.

Representative examples of these designs are engravings on five small balls of steatite stone, which in size and shape perfectly match the marbles of today's schoolboys. Since these stones were found in the grave of a boy about eight or nine years, the assupmtion is that he played with them just as boys do today. The round stones suggested to the artist the character and arrangement of his shapes. All are essentially circular, like the stone itself. The emphasis is upon graceful scrolls and circles which give the designs life and vivacity. Some shapes seem to have been derived from recognizable forms, like fantastic faces and leaves, vines and other bits of plant life. Other designs may have been made only for decoration. Even though the meaning of these engravings cannot be explained, the beauty and crispness of line, pleasing graceful shapes and balanced proportions of the designs can be appreciated. These

172

marbles must have been such proud possessions of the Indian youth that his parents carefully placed them at his side after his unfortunately early death.

Similar shapes were cut out of sheet copper. One example looks like the conventionalized tendrils and leaves of a bean plant, another more closely resembles a typical wild clover. The swastika was unexpectedly found together with these copper forms in a single cache of the

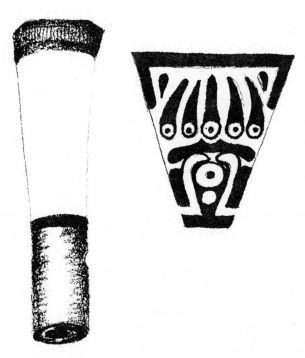

Left, a bear claw in bone and, right, bear claw in copper.

Hopewell Mound group. It is slightly different in shape from the swastika that symbolized the Nazi party during the days of Hitler. Although the swastika is a rare design in the art of the Mound Builders, it was not unknown to other ancient peoples, where it often symbolized a sun-worshiping cult. Inasmuch as the arms of this design point in four directions, it may have symbolized the four corners of the world — north, south, east and west — commonly observed in beliefs of American Indian tribes.

A bear cult may also have existed among the Hopewell. This belief is based on finds of bearlike claws cut out of copper and the portrayal of bear claws in a number of designs, such as the engraving made around a section of human bone. When the design is *unrolled,* it seems that the imprint of a bear's paw was intended. The existence of such a cult would explain the long journeys that the Hopewell Indians made to the Rocky Mountains in search of the eyeteeth and claws of the giant grizzly bear.

These various works exemplify the richness and variety of shape in the Hopewell art style. Whatever the subject, material or technique employed by these artists, all forms embody the rhythmic qualities basic to their art. Shapes undulate and move. Lines and edges are remarkably crisp and sharp. Hopewell designs are definitely not repetitious or monotonous in any way, but show a surprising diversity and originality of style.

12

The Hawk Takes Flight

WHAT became of the Mound Builders? A satisfactory answer may not be forthcoming. Did catastrophic floods, droughts or plagues destroy these peoples and the cultures they had created? Did warlike marauders invade their homeland and drive them far from the Ohio Valley? Was it for religious reasons that they deserted the villages and sacred precincts when the "Great Spirits" no longer prevailed? Could it be the belief that a cycle of human life had ended? Had evil spirits been all-powerful when this cycle of life had revolved to terminate the continuity of culture? Whatever the cause or causes may have been, and there seems no way of knowing positively what they were, both the Hopewell and Adena cultures came to an end sometime before the year A.D. 1000.

It is hard to imagine, let alone explain, how the Hopewell and Adena Indians could have vanished so abruptly from the Ohio Valley which had been their home for so many centuries. Their hypothetical trail has been traced from Asia across the Bering Strait toward the end of the Ice Age. Lured southward by more favorable climatic conditions as the ice floes retreated, they journeyed into the Ohio Valley. They progressed from small bands of nomadic hunters of wild animals to large groups of settled farmers. Many generations passed before a growing population attained the cultural climax indicated by the beautiful works of art which have been uncovered by archaeologists. Eventually they achieved a culture unsurpassed by any ancient Indian tribe east of the Rockies.

Then, apparently quite suddenly, the villages and mound sites were deserted. It was as if the inhabitants had fallen into some deep river or canyon that had closed over them. Although the people themselves sank out of sight, their artistic imprint has been traced in different directions at various times. These art forms and motifs were absorbed by many widely separated Indian tribes and served as the seed from which new styles or fashions in art were to sprout, grow and flower.

It is believed by some scholars that the Hopewell and Adena descendants were divided into several groups and spread in different directions like the Israelites of Old Testament times. They settled, it is supposed, in new places and began to build new villages like those they had left behind. Perhaps they were welcomed by the Indians they found already inhabiting the new sites and shared with them the remnants of their traditional culture. Over the course of centuries the Hopewell and Adena peoples became integrated with widely scattered tribes to whom they taught their original ways of doing things. Thus their presence has been recognized in different parts of the eastern United States.

Some of the Hopewell people may have moved northwestward up the Mississippi Valley and settled in what is now the southern part of Wisconsin. There Indians constructed earthen burial mounds in forms representing animals and birds. Archaeologists have called this culture the "Effigy Mound Culture." Based on the Carbon 14 tests of materials found in these mounds, their dates have been estimated as somewhere between A.D. 700 and A.D. 1300. It is assumed that the idea of building mounds in the shape of effigies was inspired by the Hopewell Great Serpent Mound of Ohio. The Wisconsin effigy mounds were low, seldom exceeding four feet in height, but many of them extended for hundreds of feet in length. A mound shaped like a hawk with outstretched wings measured 624 feet from one wing tip to the other. But the objects found in these graves were very limited in number and only generally reminiscent of the form or style of the Hopewell carvings.

The primitive Wisconsin tribes did not achieve the political or religious federation of the Ohio Hopewell peoples, for it is evident that their small groups were widely scattered. Some anthropologists believe that the Menomini, Dakota and Algonkian tribes, some of whose members may survive today, were direct descendants.

Other bands of Ohio Mound Builders may have moved northeast and settled in the region of what is now upper New York State. Just like their Wisconsin cousins, they also mingled with the Indians they found living there. The Angonkian Indians, who were on hand to meet the early colonists of the seventeenth century, were probably descendants of the Hopewell. The Algonkian retained such Hopewell customs as the antler-horn headdress worn by tribal priests or chieftains. The villagers arranged their hair in the same way and wore the same type of clothing as portrayed on the Hopewell figurines from the Turner Mound. Furthermore, the Algonkian artists used a style of decoration very similar to the rounded curvilinear designs of the Hopewell.

Still another group of Hopewell Indians is believed to have migrated southward and become a part of the so-called Temple Mound Culture that was spreading from the Gulf northward up the Mississippi River valley. Effigy smoking pipes, certain design motifs and techniques of working copper, shell and other materials were some of the Hopewell characteristics recognizable in the arts and crafts of the Temple Mound builders.

The delicacy and refinement of the Hopewell art soon lost its importance in the style of these later Indians, their place being taken by the heavier and more block-like forms of ancient Mexican cultures. The Temple Mound Culture is believed to have originated in the Gulf Coast region about A.D. 1000. Mexican influences have been clearly detected not only in its art but also in its ceremonial ritual and costumes. One of the most striking evidences of Mexican influence was the new shape of the earthen mounds, quite similar to those built by the Mayan and Toltec Indians. These were large truncated pyramids of earth faced with sod or rubble. They ranged up to 100 feet in height and covered several acres. Like the well-known Mexican temple pyramids, they were surmounted with shrines for sacrifices by priests. Perhaps, as some archaeologists maintain, these influences were brought to the Gulf Coast by native voyagers from the south and owed little to the northern Mound Builders. This Temple Mound Culture flourished for many generations, reaching its peak between A.D. 1300 and A.D. 1500. It was still in existence when the first Europeans appeared on the shores of the Gulf of Mexico.

When the first European explorers penetrated the Ohio Valley in the sixteenth century, the Hopewell and Adena Indians had long since disappeared. Only the monumental earthworks attested to their previous existence. The Indians living near the mounds were totally ignorant of their origin or use and of the once great culture that had flourished in the wilderness which now provided them with such an uncertain and hazardous livelihood.

The mystery of the Mound Builders has fascinated Americans since the time the mounds were first discovered. A solution of this mystery will not be forthcoming until more mounds are scientifically investigated, and more evidence is recovered by experienced archaeologists, backed by trained geologists and anthropologists and aided by engineers, museum experts and other interested scholars.

Then the flight of the hawk through the heavens will have new symbolism and significance as its shadow falls over the green fields and rolling hills, the meandering streams and broad superhighways, the quiet villages and the bustling cities, that have supplanted the ancient Mound Builders in the rich Ohio Valley.

Selected Bibliography

Cole, Fay-Cooper, and Deuel, Thorne
  1937. *Rediscovering Illinois.* Chicago.
Cooper, L. R.
  1933. *Red Cedar Variant of the Wisconsin Hopewell Culture.*
  Bulletin of the Public Museum of the City of Milwaukee,
  Vol. 16, No. 2.
Deuel, Thorne, editor
  1952. *Hopewellian Communities in Illinois.* Scientific Papers,
  Vol. V, Springfield.
Fischel, Hans E.
  1939. "Folsom and Yuma Culture Finds." *American Antiquity.*
  Vol. 4, No. 3, Menasha.
Ford, James A., and Quimby, George I., Jr.
  1945. *The Tchefuncte Culture.* Society for Archaeology, Mem-
  oir No. 2, Menasha.
Greenman, Emerson F.
  1932. "Excavation of the Coon Mound and an Analysis of the
  Adena Culture." *Ohio Archaeological and Historical Quarterly,* Vol. 41, No. 3, pp. 369-410, Columbus.
Griffin, James B.
  1943. *The Fort Ancient Aspect, Its Cultural and Chronologi-
  cal Position in Mississippi Valley Archaeology,* Ann Arbor.

Griffin, James B., editor
1952. *Archaeology of the Eastern United States.* Chicago.

Johnson, Frederick, et al.
1949. *The Boylston Street Fishweir, II.* Papers of the Robert S. Peabody Foundation for Archaeology, Vol. 4, No. 1, Andover.

Johnson, Frederick, assembler
1951. *Radiocarbon Dating.* Society for American Anthropology, Memoir No. 8, Salt Lake City.

Knoblock, Byron W.
1939. *Bannerstones of the North American Indian.* La Grange.

Lewis, T. M. N., and Kneberg, Madeline
1947. *The Archaic Horizon in Western Tennessee.* Tennessee Anthropology Papers, No. 2, The University of Tennessee Record, Extension Series, Vol. 23, No. 4, Knoxville.

McKern, W. C.
1931. *A Wisconsin Variant of the Hopewell Culture.* Bulletin of the Public Museum of the City of Milwaukee, Vol. 10, No. 2.

McKern, W. C., Titterington, Paul F., and Griffin, James B.
1945. "Painted Pottery Figurines From Illinois." *American Antiquity,* Vol. 10, No. 3, pp. 295-302, Menasha.

Martin, Paul S., Quimby, George I., Jr., and Collier, Donald
1947. *Indians Before Columbus.* Chicago.

Mills, William C.
1902. "Excavation of the Adena Mound." *Ohio Archaeological and Historical Quarterly,* Vol. 10, No. 4, pp. 452-479, Columbus.
1907. "The Explorations of the Edwin Harness Mound." *Ohio Archaeological and Historical Quarterly,* Vol. 16, No. 2, pp. 113-193, Columbus.
1909. "Explorations of the Seip Mound." *Ohio Archaeological and Historical Quarterly,* Vol. 18, pp. 269-321, Columbus.
1916. "Explorations of the Tremper Mound." *Ohio Archaeological and Historical Quarterly,* Vol. 25, No. 3, pp. 269-398, Columbus.

1922. "Exploration of the Mound City Group." *Ohio Archaeological and Historical Quarterly,* Vol. 31, No. 4, pp. 423-584, Columbus.

1922. "Exploration of the Mound City Group." In *Certain Mounds and Village Sites in Ohio,* Vol. 3, No. 4, pp. 245-406, Columbus.

Moorehead, Warren K.

1922. "The Hopewell Mound Group of Ohio." *Field Museum of Natural History,* Publication 211, Anthropology Series, Vol. 6, No. 5, Chicago.

Quimby, George I., Jr.

1960. *Indian Life in the Upper Great Lakes.* Chicago.

Ritchie, William A.

1944. *The Pre-Iroquoian Occupation of New York State.* Rochester Museum of Arts and Sciences, Memoir No. 1.

Setzler, Frank M.

1933. "Pottery of the Hopewell Type from Louisiana." *Proceedings of the United States National Museum,* Vol. 82, Article 22, Washington.

Shetrone, Henry C.

1926. "Explorations of the Hopewell Group of Prehistoric Earthworks." *Ohio Archaeological and Historical Quarterly,* Vol. 35, No. 1 pp. 1-227, Columbus.

1930. *The Mound Builders.* New York.

Shetrone, Henry C., and Greenman, Emerson F.

1931. "Exploration of the Seip Group of Prehistoric Earthworks." *Ohio Archaeological and Historical Quarterly,* Vol. 40, No. 3, pp. 343-509, Columbus.

Squierm, Ephram G., and Davis, Edwin H.

1848. *Ancient Monuments of the Mississippi Valley.* Smithsonian Contributions to Knowledge, Vol. 1, Washington.

Webb, William S.

1940. *The Wright Mounds.* The University of Kentucky Reports in Anthropology, Vol. 5, No. 1, Lexington.

1942. *The C and O Mounds at Paintsville.* The University of Kentucky Reports in Anthropology, Vol. 5, No. 4. Lexington.

1946. *Indian Knoll*. The University of Kentucky Reports in Anthropology, Vol. 4, No. 3, Part 1, Lexington.

1950. *The Carlson Annis Mound*. The University of Kentucky Reports in Anthropology, Vol. 7, No. 4, Lexington.

1947. *Archaic Sites in McLean County*. The University of Kentucky Reports in Anthropology, Vol. 7, No. 1, Lexington.

Webb, William S., and Snow, Charles E.

1945. *The Adena People*. The University of Kentucky Reports in Anthropology, Vol. 6, Lexington.

Webb, William S., and Baby, Raymond S.

1957. *The Adena People No. 2*. Ohio Archaeological and Historical Quarterly, Columbus.

West, George A.

1934. *Tobacco, Pipes and Smoking Customs of the American Indians*. Bulletin of the Public Museum of the City of Milwaukee, Vol. 17.

Willoughby, Charles C., and Hooton, Earnest A.

1922. *The Turner Group of Earthworks*. Papers of the Peabody Museum of Archaeology and Ethnology, Vol. 8, No. 3, Cambridge.

Wormington, Helen M.

1949. *Ancient Man in North America*. Denver Museum of Natural History, Popular Series, No. 4, third edition, Denver.

Chronology

	NORTH AMERICA	MEXICO SOUTH AMERICA	EUROPE MEDITERRANEAN
A.D.			
1800			French Revolution
	American		
1700	colonization		
	historic tribes		
1600			
1500	Temple Mound	colonization by	
	Indians	Spain	Renaissance
1300	Pueblo Indians	Inca, Aztec,	
		Maya civilizations	
1000			
	Hopewell Indians		
750	Adena Indians	Toltec civilization	Middle Ages
500			
			Fall of the
			Roman Empire
100			
			Birth of Christ
B.C.			
100			
			Age of Pericles
500		Maya civilization	Roman Republic
1000	Hopewell Indians		Homer
	Adena Indians		
			Egyptian pyramids
5000	Archaic Indians		
10,000			
20,000	Early Hunters		Cave Man
	First Immigrants		
30,000	to New World		
40,000			
50,000			

185

Index

Crater Lake, Oregon, 27

Davis, E. H., 82
Denver Museum of Natural History, 21
Diomedes Islands, 25
Duck Hawk, 122, 125, 126, 133-38, 140-44, 146, 147, 149, 150, 152-57, 159, 162, 163
 carvings and variations of, 134-38, 140, 142-44, 146, 147, 149, 150, 152-57
 different species of, 134
 evolutions of, 141
 as symbols to Indians, 133, 134, 140

Early Hunter, 23, 25-30, 32, 67
Early man, 21-23, 25-30, 32
Effigy Mound Culture, 177
Egyptian pyramids, 77
Empire State Building, 75
European explorers, 46, 179

Figgins, Dr. J. D., 21-23
Florida, 99
Folsom, New Mexico, 21, 23
Folsom Man, 23
Folsom spearpoints, 23, 25
Fort Ancient, 76, 77

Grave Creek Mound, 79-81
Great bisons, 27
Great Earthwork Builders, 78
Great Lakes region, 60
Great Plains, 26
"Great Spirits," 175
Green River, 32

Hopewell Indians, 28, 58, 60, 64, 69-72, 75-79, 83-85, 88-90, 93-96, 98, 100-03, 105-09, 115-17, 120, 121, 123, 124, 127-29, 135, 136, 138, 140, 143, 149, 155, 157, 162, 171, 172, 174-79
 bear cult, 174
 culture, 70, 71, 78, 93, 100, 115, 116, 118, 175
 Mound Group, 72, 104, 136, 146, 162, 164, 174

(southern) Illinois mound site, 78, 108, 113
Kansas mound site, 79
Louisiana mound, 96, 144, 150
(southern) Ohio mound site, 70-72, 75-79, 85, 96, 98, 120, 177
Oklahoma mound site, 79
Wisconsin mound site, 79, 177
Horned monster, 168-71
Horned Serpent, 168, 169
Human forms, rare examples of, 164
Hunting Falcon, 134

Ice Age, 25, 31, 32, 44, 163, 176
Illinois River, 78, 108
India, 33
Indiana, 79
Indians, 25-29, 32-35, 38, 39, 45, 46, 61, 63, 64, 66-68, 72, 79, 82-85, 100, 104, 113, 116, 120, 121, 123, 127, 130, 133-35, 137, 140-42, 144, 159, 162, 163, 166, 168, 169, 171, 176-78
Iowa, 25
Isle Royale, 61
Israelites, 176

Jefferson, Thomas, 81, 82

Kanawha River, 79
Kentucky, 79
Keweenaw Peninsula, 61
Knight Mound, 108-10, 112, 113, 115

Lake Superior region, 60, 64, 99
Libby, Dr. Willard F., 33
Little Miami River, 71
Long Island, 25

Mayan Indians, 178
Mediterranean, 33
Meigs tablet, 150, 153
Mesopotamia, 33
Mexico, 26, 67, 79, 99, 113, 168
Middle Ages, 100, 134
Mississippi River, 32, 70
Mississippi Valley, 60, 68, 177
Mongoloid people, 23
Mound, procedure of opening a, 83, 84

Mound Builders, 30, 32, 65, 66, 82, 83, 104, 115, 117, 130, 134, 141, 163, 174-76
mystery of, 175-79
Mound City Group, 72, 119, 128, 142, 146, 164, 167
Moundsville, 79
Museum of Modern Art, 141

National Research Council, 83
New Mexico, 23, 27
New York State (upper), 177
Niagara Falls, 27
Nicot, Jean, 44
Nicotiana, 44
North America, 21, 22, 25, 26, 31, 32, 70, 72, 85, 171

Ohio River, 32, 70-72, 79, 164, 175
Ohio Valley, 23, 32, 39, 40, 44, 46, 60, 67, 68, 76, 79, 81, 84, 93, 99, 113, 115, 128, 136, 155, 175, 176, 179
Old Copper Indians, 61, 63, 64
culture of, 61, 64
Old World, 61, 82

Peebles, 75
Peregrine Falcon, 134
Plant life, designs derived from, 171-73
Portsmouth, 120
Proper Mound Building archaeology, 82, 86-89

Rio Grande, 132, 136, 168

Scioto River, 71, 72, 79
Seip Mound Group, 72, 164

Serpent Mound, 58, 75-77, 169, 177
Shell-mound people, 32-35, 40
Smithsonian Institution, 82
Spanish conquistadors, 156
Squier, E. G., 82
Subway construction (1913), 35
Sucker fish, 167
Swastika, 173, 174

Tarascan Indians, 113, 136
artists of, 115, 132, 155
culture of, 113
Temple Mound builders, 178
culture of, 178, 179
origin of culture, 178
Tennessee River, 32
Texas, 26
Tierra del Fuego, 26
Toltec Indians, 178
Tomb Builders, culture of, 64
Tremper Mound, 72, 93, 119, 120
Trumpeter swan, 164, 166
Turner Mound Group, 72, 88, 89, 93, 104, 108, 109, 159, 164, 168

United States, 21, 25, 29, 64, 177

Wabash River, 32
West Virginia, 79
Willoughby, Charles, 104, 105
Wilmington, 76
Wilmington tablet, 150, 152, 153
Wisconsin tribes, 177
World War II, 33
Wright tablet, 150

Yellowstone Park, 99

The Author

After receiving his Ph.D. in Art History and Archaeology from the Ohio State University, Robert Myron joined the faculty of Hofstra. His fascination with the Indian Mound Builders began when he first viewed the vast collection of artifacts and sculpture in the Ohio State Museum. From that time, Mr. Myron has accumulated countless notes and participated in innumerable "digs." He has written one other book, *Prehistoric Art*.

The author lives with his wife and two sons, Daniel and Jacques, in a small house near the edge of the Hofstra campus.